# Fifty-Five Fathers

## Real Men Share Their Stories and Life Lessons about Their Own Fathers

### JEFF PAISLEY

*Fifty-Five Fathers: Real Men Share Their Stories and Life Lessons about Their Own Fathers*

Published by Wheatmark™
610 East Delano Street, Suite 104
Tucson, Arizona 85705 U.S.A.
www.wheatmark.com

International Standard Book Number: 978-1-58736-957-5
Library of Congress Control Number: 2007935558

When I was a boy of fourteen, my father was so ignorant I could hardly stand to have the old man around. But when I got to be twenty-one, I was astonished at how much the old man had learned in seven years.

Mark Twain, father of three

# Dedication

This is dedicated to Dad, Gramps, Grandpa, Mom, Granny, Grandma, Reed, Al, Howie, Scott, Stinky, J Dad, the Fifty-Five and their fathers, Mary, and to all dads everywhere.

And a huge thank you to my editors/proof-readers: CJ, Ruben, Steve, Kathy, Hayley, Grael, and Mary.

# Contents

✪ = Relatives are grouped together

# Why

My father passed away too many years ago. After the worst had happened, I'd been thinking of him so often and deeply that it led me to wondering how he had affected my take on everything. You know, boys and their dads.

I started asking my male friends about their fathers, soaking up their stories, to see if my own would become any clearer. Those stories were so wonderful, varied, funny, and profound, that they really struck a chord inside me. So I recorded the interviews of Fifty-Five men as they answered the same ten questions about their fathers (p. xiii). Collecting these stories as a book is my opportunity to share these real men, their memories, and their fathers.

After the first few interviews, I realized I'd become the keeper of these stories. As I finished transcribing each man's Chapter, I gave him copies of the audio interview and written Chapter to share with his family; some interviews even contained information that was unknown to family members. These stories continue to sneak up and present themselves, particularly when I encounter similar situations.

Many of the Fifty-Five men (the Fifty-Five) told me that if they had more time to think and prepare, they would have had a great deal more to say and many more stories to tell. Some of the Fifty-Five did answer the questions out of order, which might have given them a quick chance to reorganize their thoughts. Often, other pieces of memories came out while they searched their minds for a different, specific one. But as Johnny discovered, I wanted each of the men to respond with his first true thought, that initial push of brain waves that finds the strongest feeling answer.

All of our stories continue to change. Since their interviews, two of the Fifty-Five have lost their fathers. One included pieces from his interview in his eulogy to his dad.

My vision is that the ideas and experiences of the Fifty-Five will help men and women and families talk with each other more, spend more important time together, continually think of new questions to ask each other, and then ask them. My deepest gratitude goes out to the Fifty-Five for their interviews and time. I hope these stories connect. I have more. Maybe next time I can talk with you.

# How

I have met a lot of interesting guys while living in a big city and working in a big company. The men interviewed for this book are friends and acquaintances. Most of the men knew I was doing a book about fathers before the interview, but only two knew the questions beforehand. The ages of the Fifty-Five are from eighteen to eighty and all decades in between. The ethnic backgrounds of the men reflect the 2000 US Census findings, but it is not a scientific or a representative sample: 71 percent white, 11 percent Black, 11 percent Hispanic, 4 percent Asian, 1 percent American Indian, and 2 percent other.

All interviews were conducted face-to-face, and are presented with specific attention to accuracy, vocal rhythms, and standard usage. My answers are also included as one of The Fifty-Five; the first draft was done before I had conducted any interviews.

I used an older ipod as my voice recorder and listened to the original audio clips while transcribing the first draft of the Chapters on the computer; Mary Paisley did first draft transcriptions of seven interviews and was the photographer of the front and back cover pictures. The ten questions are listed as numbers only after the first ten Chapters. A complete list of the ten questions is on page xiii.

Words in parentheses are my descriptions and came about because of laughter; almost every one of the Fifty-Five laughed during his interview. Laughter is very important to the rhythms of speaking. Laughter creates a pause for the speaker and listener to think.

It can also be a nervous reaction or a comment on the seriousness of the topic. Laughter can even soften the blow of what's said next. The Fifty-Five laughed numerous times in all these styles.

Each interview began with me reading:

*I am doing a book about fathers and I'd like to include your interview. I'll ask you ten questions and record your answers for the book. Your answers will be presented as spoken, with minor editing.*

*You will be identified only by your self-chosen, interview first name and your real age.*

Then I asked each man the same ten questions.

# The Ten Questions

1. *What is your interview name and your real age?*

2. *By what name do you call your father, Dad, Papa, and how did you arrive at that name?*

3. *How would people describe your father? Do you agree?*

4. *Tell a story of your father teaching you a skill.*

5. *Share an incident you experienced when you were proud of your father.*

6. *Tell something you picked up or got from your father.*

7. *Tell a favorite story about your dad.*

8. *What's something you discovered later in life about your father that surprised you?*

9. *Describe a particularly clear memory of being with your father.*

10. *What single trait or strength should all fathers own?*

# CHAPTER 1

# Lee

*1. What is your interview name and your real age?*

Lee, sixty-four.

*2. By what name do you call your father, Dad, Papa, and how did you arrive at that name?*

Dad. I guess that was because my older brother called him Dad so I always called him Dad.

*3. How would people describe your father?*

Well, he was very creative, but a very unpredictable type guy. Made a lot of money, lost a lot of money, and never felt that he couldn't make it again.

*Do you agree?*

Yeah, that's pretty true.

*4. Tell a story of your father teaching you a skill.*

He worked all the time in his drugstore. So often, teaching skills was left to my mom; but he was interested in me learning how to play baseball and taught me how to throw and catch the ball and things like that.

*5. Share an incident you experienced when you were proud of your father.*

My dad, he always liked people. He was the pharmacist. And on several occasions during his life, he knew somebody was sick and didn't have any money, and he'd give them the money or medicine that they needed so they could get well or eat. He was a very benevolent type of person.

*6. Tell something you picked up or got from your father.*

He did everything with a gusto. If you're going to be a pharmacist, be the best pharmacist. He was very creative. He didn't let rules or society bug him one way or the other. What he thought he wanted to do was what he did. He didn't worry about what somebody else thought.

*7. Tell a favorite story about your dad.*

I have a bunch of them. The favorite story, he was oldest of eleven kids, and we were back in Arkansas. And how free he was to express himself depended on whether he was drinking Jack Daniels at the time or not.

But, there was a family picnic; I don't know what holiday it was. They went out on this creek in Arkansas and there was a pond there. It must have been more summer time, so it wasn't Christmas, must have been Easter, and he had to run the drug store downtown in this small Arkansas town. He came in this three-piece brown suit and had nice shoes on.

Some of the kids had been jumping in this watering hole and they started teasing him and stuff. And he said, " I can go in swimming."

And they said, "No, you can't. You'll get your suit all dirty."

And he just jumped in the pond and said, "See I can do anything I want." (Laughs.)

*8. What's something you discovered later in life about your father that surprised you?*

When I was younger, he was so off the cuff, and my mother being very conservative, he sometimes sort of spooked me. When I got older, I thought his creativity, spontaneity, and his love of life was needed, important, and I felt very comfortable with it.

*9. Describe a particularly clear memory of being with your father.*

While I was getting my Masters' Degree, we were living in a small town in Arkansas and I was going to Arkansas State University. We were right by this huge river, so we kept our fishing poles and a boat down by the river.

So he said, "Well, let's go fishing. I'm off today." And I was out of school so we went down and got the boat and we went out on what they call in the South, a cut-off. Means the river changes course so it leaves a channel of water but it's not as swift as the main river. And he didn't really care too much about fishing, he just wanted to get out and spend some time. (Laughs.)

We were fishing this day and we were catching all these perch and we caught eight or nine fish and we had them on a hook stringer. All of a sudden, the water started shaking beside the boat, and he reached down and started pulling that chain up with the fish on it and he pulled it over in the boat. And there was about a four-foot water moccasin stuck on that thing!

And I stood up at the other end of the boat; I was ready to go. And Dad had been sipping on some Old Yellowstone, and he usually wore multiple bifocals; he couldn't see real well without his glasses. But he held that chain up and took the paddle out of the boat and swung and hit that water moccasin in the head and put a crease in it. It rolled over dead. And I was still standing at the other end of the boat ready to jump in case he missed the snake.

And he reached down with paddle, flipped the snake up and said, "I didn't want that snake to get our fish." (Laughs.)

*10. What single trait or characteristic should all fathers own?*

We are all individual, different types of people. And we have to relate in our way. And most fathers do. As long as you let the child know that you love them, care about them, and allow them to become the person they are going to be, you'll be a good father.

My advice to all men upon choosing a female partner: "Always find out how the woman feels about her own father. That will give you a good indication of how she feels about men in general."

# CHAPTER 2

# Vic

*1. What is your interview name and your real age?*

(Laughs.) I'll be Vic Vega. Eighteen.

*2. By what name do you call your father, Dad, Papa, and how did you arrive at that name?*

It's funny; we both address each other as Man.

"Hey Man, what's up. Where you going?" Or Dad. Dude. Kind of informal stuff like that. Old Man.

There's no real landmark event where it started. It's natural. It was natural.

*3. How would people describe your father?*

Everybody that has talked to me about him usually describes him as this funny, loud guy. You know, cares a lot. He's kind to everybody. Looks out for you and stuff.

*And you agree with that?*

Yes.

*4. Tell a story of your father teaching you a skill.*

I have a lot of memories of him teaching me how to build things in general—how to work with wood, how to work with metal, how to apply paint to things, how to sculpt stuff.

I remember we used to do a lot of wood projects when I was

younger. We'd build a doghouse or a bird feeder. Dad taught me a lot about building things, fixing things.

*5. Share an incident you experienced when you were proud of your father.*

Early, when he went back to college again, he enrolled and then decided to drop out and go do roofing because it was a lot of fast money. He just got tired of it and decided he was going to back to school and do something else.

He went back through college and got his degree in Early Childhood Education. And that's what he's doing now. And ever since then, I've just seen him as a self-made man. He had an idea and he went out and did it. He did it for himself, by himself, and that's really cool. I think about it a lot.

*6. Tell something you picked up or got from your father.*

Mechanical skills, he's taught me pretty much everything. How to mess with wiring. Any sort of mechanical skill, probably I've gotten from him. It's not really stuff you are born knowing or you learn on your own.

*7. Tell a favorite story about your dad.*

He tore his ACL bowling. I always make fun of him because of that—he fell. It's not that great of a story.

There was this time; I don't even remember what we were doing or what happened. It was something he told me. I've really thought about it a lot. It was a piece of fatherly advice.

He told me, "If you are going to do something half-assed, you might as well not do it at all." Which seems to get more important as I get older, and I think about that more because of all the meanings it has. It means to not get over-loaded to the point of instead of doing really good work on a few things; you do really poor work on many things. It says to me you should care about what you're doing. If you're not putting all you have into what you're doing, you're wasting your time.

That's one thing I've just really lived my whole life by. If you're going to half-ass something, just don't do it. It's not going to be your best work.

*8. What's something you discovered later in life about your father that surprised you?*

Probably just how similar we are. As I got older, I realized as I entered high school and he started talking about what he did in high school, he started to seem more like me. I've always loved my dad, but in a sense, he became more human because of the similarities.

*9. Describe a particularly clear memory of being with your father.*

There's this beach outside L.A. called Doc Wiler. My dad's from Arizona, but my mom's from the L.A. area of California and we're always going down there. Pretty much every Fourth of July since the beginning of time, until the time I was about thirteen, we were there, just playing football in the sand, and barbecuing and stuff. Setting off fireworks, that's fun because fireworks are legal in California so we'd play with those. He taught me how to set off fireworks properly; it's a good skill. I don't know, there's just this really ephemeral quality. I mean the summer nights on Doc Wiler, just in being there, that's always with me.

*10. What single trait or characteristic should all fathers own?*

I think that you should be able to talk to them. The thing that I like the most about my dad is that I can communicate with him. He listens and doesn't just automatically react to whatever you say. He'll actually think about it before he puts in. I think you should be able to talk to your dad. Because if you can't, who can you talk to?

# CHAPTER 3

# Johnny

*1. What is your interview name and your real age?*

I'm sixty-four and you can call me Johnny.

*2. By what name do you call your father, Dad, Papa, and how did you arrive at that name?*

Wouldn't remember how I arrived at it, and I would have called him Dad.

*3. How would people describe your father?*

Probably good natured, and a hard worker.

*Do you agree with that?*

Oh yeah. I would have said that all along.

*4. Tell a story of your father teaching you a skill.*

Well maybe not so much one instance. My dad was a machinist, and all the time that he was at home, there was always some work to be done; he would always be fixing something. So I was going to school all the time. Learning how to do this, learning how to do that, or maybe learning how to not do that because he was very vocal and vocal with four letter words. And those people who know me, know that I don't use them. I think it's because I always found that when Dad would start to use four letter words, he was not making any headway in repairing what he was repairing. So

I don't use the language. That way I think I'm achieving the goal quicker.

*5. Share an incident you experienced when you were proud of your father.*

Well, there are probably lots of those. There was an instance where he handled something and he kind of let me off the hook when I thought I was going to be in big trouble—I like that. It wasn't something he did in front of a whole lot of other people, so I was just pleased that he was able to do it that way.

I had been out drag racing my car on side streets, which in Los Angeles was pretty common. Now that I'm as old as I am, I realize it's not the smartest thing to do. But, when I went to second gear, I lost the transmission. Then I got it home and got it in the back yard and my dad was going to help me find out why the transmission was broken. When we drained the transmission, out came one of the teeth from second gear. And as he examined it, he said, "Well, looks like this has been about half broke before. Boy you're lucky it lasted as long as it did." It wasn't like I was out drag racing and did something bad.

Then he said, "It was already a poor part and it just finally failed on you." So I thought good, he let me off the hook there. It was better than him giving me a really bad time about doing stuff I shouldn't do. The lesson was the same; only I learned an extra lesson at the same time.

*6. Tell something you picked up or got from your father.*

I actually got my patience from my father because he didn't have much patience. So I suppose that would be the way to say that. It's one of those things where you learn what not to do by watching others.

*7. Tell a favorite story about your dad.*

Most of our stories were not positive kinds of stories. But I do like one, which might be hard to put the humor to; I have even told this a number of times before. After he had retired, we took a trip to Lake Havasu, and out on the island, which had been developed by then, there's a campground on the upstream part of the Colorado River. And we went up there and we set up camp.

We needed to rent a boat because we wanted to fish up there and we didn't have a boat. So we drove across, near the nautical end, to rent a boat. And since we had the car on the other side of the island from where we were renting the boat, my dad decided he would drive the boat back around the island to the campground, while we would drive the car the quick, short distance back to the campground and wait for him to come around the island. And then we'd all throw in the fishing gear and go fishing.

And we waited awhile. It actually turned out that it was just a little aluminum boat with a thirty-five horsepower motor and it took a while for that to go all around the outside of the island because the perimeter was much farther than we anticipated. But when he came around and into view, he started straight across the lake to a point that was about a mile and a half up river from where we were. He was just disoriented as to how far he'd gone, so we sat and watched him go across the lake.

He was about the only one out there in a little aluminum fishing boat, chugging along with the determined process, but going the wrong way. So I went down and waded in the water; there was a guy with one of those big Biesemeyer speedboats and he was just cranking up the engine. And I pointed out to the middle of the lake and said, "That's my dad out there and he's got a little disoriented and he doesn't know where we are." So I asked the guy to give me a ride and he did. And I jumped in that boat and he cranked up the engine and headed out straight for that little, aluminum, fishing boat.

And when we pulled up alongside my dad, he looked over at this guy; I don't think he saw me right away because he was wondering why this big old three hundred horsepower boat was trying to run him out of the lake. And then when he saw me sitting there he was really puzzled like, what are you doing on that boat? It was awhile before I got transferred into the aluminum boat and

I pointed him back in the right direction. It was interesting, something we remember, one of our little mini-vacations.

*8. What's something you discovered later in life about your father that surprised you?*

Religion, that's an easy one. When my sisters and I were growing up, especially my little sister who was only a year, eighteen months younger, we were always strongly encouraged to go to church, which we did. And neither my mom nor my dad would go regularly or if ever. Maybe they were the Easter churchgoers.

And it wasn't until he passed away actually—I found out when the minister had come by. My mother had asked him to come over and they started talking about my dad and began to set up the services and what they wanted to say at the service and things like that. My mom and my brother-in-law, who had been living nearby and had spent the last eight years really close to my family and my dad, the two of them stood right up and talked to the minister about how Dad was very religious.

And that caught me by real surprise. We never had conversations with him in that regard. Of course by then, I wasn't going to have a conversation with him.

*9. Describe a particularly clear memory of being with your father.*

Well there's a bunch of those. Your format of asking the questions is kind of interesting because we don't have time. I mean these are like what pops into your mind first thing. So it's not like you can think back and have, perhaps, a larger, better example.

But vacation trips, vacation weekends were when my dad and I would get together and spend any, what we would call now, quality time. But our trips were always a little haphazard. There was always something that seemed to go wrong.

And on the one occasion I'm thinking of right now, we just went down to the ocean and went out on a pier. Again we didn't have a boat. We didn't even have fishing gear, so we rented a salt water fishing rig and we walked way out on the stone breakwater. And there were a lot of other people out there fishing. We got about half way out there and he decided that's a good place to try fishing, so we sat down, and got all the gear set up. He reared back and cast that line out into the water and threw that whole rented rig out into the ocean.

So (Laughs), we didn't do much fishing that day.

The memory of my dad was that he was a hard working fellow; it never got him too far as far as owning things because he never had money for that. And then on the occasions that he tried to get away from work and go and have a good time, maybe splurge a little bit by renting a boat or renting a fishing reel and rod, something went wrong. So it was never a disaster. But it was always a little bit of a disappointment, or at least a unique experience.

*10. What single trait or characteristic should all fathers own?*

I've been reading different books lately and a lot of what's been going through my mind has been these books, novels. Generally what I've been reading about is the disconnect from home life, which is bad. I suspect if you are looking for traits that fathers would have, then it would be that they have more connection to home life, to being there with the family. Being a part of the family, not just doing their piece of it, which generally is stereotyped as they get up in the morning and they go to work. And they make sure the mortgage is paid, and the car payment's paid, and the insurance is paid. But the wife, in this stereotype that we've had for so long, takes care of the rest of the things.

I think it's more of a connection, spending time with the kids, and the wife, and the family. Now at sixty-four, I was thinking about the family that I was part of raising, even this morning. Being in the kids' lives and daily routine seemed awfully important.

# CHAPTER 4

# James Louis

*1. What is your interview name and your real age?*

My Interview name is James Louis and my real age is thirty-four.

*2. By what name do you call your father, Dad, Papa, and how did you arrive at that name?*

I call him Dad. As long as I can remember, I have always called him Dad. It might be from hearing him calling his father, Dad, using that phrase. And I think it's just a real common way to refer to your dad, might even be a Midwest thing. It just seems like that's how I've always heard it.

*3. How would people describe your father?*

Very kind person. Very friendly. Easily makes friends with people. Tries to be humorous, doesn't always get there, but tries. He's especially good at first impressions; I think they always take him for someone they can talk to easily and be real comfortable around.

*Do you agree?*

For the most part, but of course, it's not the first impression when you're the son, you know a little bit more. So I would go a little deeper. The easy going can sometimes be frustrating. Just like anything else, sometimes the friendliness can be more superficial than real. I don't think there's an insincerity to it, but I think sometimes you're looking for something a little deeper. But I'll get frustrated with some of the things other people might just take for a nice, friendly guy.

*4. Tell a story of your father teaching you a skill.*

Probably one of the first ones I remember is him teaching me how to fish. My dad's a huge, huge fisherman. His dad fished.

I remember trying to learn how to cast and especially bait a hook—being able to put the worm on the hook or the minnow on the hook—which does take a ton of skill. (Laughs.) And I just remember poking my finger and getting frustrated with that and not wanting to do it, and of course having him do it half the time. But I remember these vivid images of me finally doing it, getting the worm on the hook so it doesn't fall off, getting the minnow on the hook so it doesn't fall off. That was a big part of it, that and being able to know how to cast it out there without hooking somebody in the boat or it not going more than two feet. Fishing played a pretty big role in our lives early on, as far as the father/son thing.

*5. Share an incident you experienced when you were proud of your father.*

There's a couple that come to mind, but let's stick on the fishing thing, because that's my train of thought. He belonged to Bassmasters, a fishing federation, and he would go out every few weeks and they would have fishing tournaments and stuff like that.

He would sometimes do pretty well, sometimes not. But there's one time I remember him winning the biggest fish part of it, called a lunker. I must have been a real little kid. He had this huge bass, six, seven pounds I think, and I just remember there were quite a few people in this bass federation. And everyone was watching as they weighed his fish and it ended up being the biggest fish and he got the trophy. And I remember how happy he was and everyone was looking at him. I remember being a little kid and thinking that must be the coolest thing in the world, right there.

The other was I always knew my dad played basketball, but it would just be stories here and there. I remember the first time I was at my grandpa's house, my dad's father. We found one of his old scrapbooks and were looking through it and all of a sudden there was a picture of Dad in his college basketball uniform. He said he'd played college basketball but I just kind of realized—you played college basketball! That was a pretty big deal. And I was like, dang, you must have been pretty good to play that. And suddenly it just kind of clicked.

*6. Tell something you picked up or got from your father.*

Hair. I got his hair, which is a good thing. He has a bit of a receding hairline, but it hangs in there. My grandpa, who lived until he was ninety-five, still had a head of hair. That's not bad.

Voice. You listen to Dad on his cell phone answering service and, oh my God it sounds like me, exactly. It's creepy how much the voices are the same.

I think I try to avoid conflict as much as I can. I don't like being confrontational and I know my dad's like that. My mom can be confrontational; it's one of her traits that she can come right out and say things. I think with my dad, he'd rather just kind of grin and bare it, just take it.

So if I'm unhappy about something, I tend to have to really work at me being assertive about it. It doesn't come naturally. It doesn't feel comfortable. I notice that, so I really work at it. Because sometimes you just flat out have to be assertive. But my instinct is to just avoid it at all costs, avoid conflict at all costs. Whether it's people mad at each other, whether it's something with work, I just would rather not have to deal with it. And I think for my dad, same thing. And I think, for better or worse, that's hurt him in a lot of ways but I also think that's helped how he smoothed over some situations. Especially if you're trying to raise three kids that are at each other's throats all the time, you probably have to have a little bit of that.

Dovetailing from that is the idea that you hope that everyone is having fun, and enjoying themselves. You don't want people to be displeased and that sort of thing. It bugs me when you know someone's not really having fun—you want to try and find out why.

And I think that's my dad, too. I don't think he's confrontational because he doesn't want to delve into that.

*7. Tell a favorite story about your dad.*

One of them is not a favorite story because it's not a joyful occasion, but because it is an occasion where I connected with my dad. His father had recently passed away. And he lived in a different city and we had to go up to the house and get it ready to be sold. The whole family couldn't go, so just my dad and me went up there.

This was probably one of the first times where my dad and I traveled up there just by ourselves, away from the family to deal with an adult situation. I was treated more as an adult and he was dealing with something that obviously was pretty emotional for him.

I just helped him with the house and we stayed overnight there. No intrusions whatsoever, just him and me. So it sits in my head almost like a sentimental thing. It wasn't a happy occasion, but I think what came from it was we became closer at that point. So it really sits in my mind that way.

*8. What's something you discovered later in life about your father that surprised you?*

For a lot of guys, it's the first time you realize that your dad is human, he's not Superman or something. For me, it was the first time I saw him cry. It was at his father's funeral and we were at the cemetery and he just broke down there. I had no idea how to react. I still can't even remember what I did, but it was that all of a sudden realization that, oh my God, my dad was a real person. I don't think I'd ever seen him cry up to that point. I never saw him as someone who could be hurt in that sense. So that was a real big awakening for me.

I think that goes for a lot of boys. You assume that your dad is always invulnerable. I was around nine or ten. The image sticks in my mind, real strong, seeing that happen. I don't even remember what I did. I don't think I knew what to do, so I just stood there. I think my mom went over and hugged him. It was just like, dang. He's crying. Wow. I think at that point you realize, dang, if he can cry, boy, we're all vulnerable now. So that was a pretty huge one.

Another one is actually relatively recent. My mom and dad picked up and moved from their home of twenty-some years, really took a chance, and moved somewhere completely different. My dad wanted to try something new and started his own business. It's worked out really well for him; he's very successful, probably busier than he wants to be. He's near retirement but it was one of those things where my dad was supporting the family, taking care of business, taking care of kids and stuff. And once the kids were out, they took a chance. And it's a chance a lot of people wouldn't take.

It worked out for them. I never realized he was such an entrepreneur—he really wanted to. He owned a business one time early in his life, when I was very young, so I really didn't know about it. Then he worked for a few companies. And then boom, he's got his own business, his own product. I just never realized that he was that interested in going out on his own and seeing what he could do. I thought that was kind of cool. It would be another one of those where I really got a sense of pride because that's kind of cool and because I kind of always wanted to do that sort of stuff and I didn't realize that he had that same feeling.

*9. Describe a particularly clear memory of being with your father.*

The first one that came to my head is kind of a depressing one—a very vivid time when we were hunting together in Minnesota. It was cold and it was icy—it's brutal, deer hunting in Minnesota.

We walked to his deer stand. I stood there to help him before I walked up a little further to get to mine. He was climbing up into the tree to get into the deer stand. I was holding onto his gun and he got almost all the way up into the deer stand, but because the ice had cracked, he slipped and he fell. He literally fell right in front of me, almost on top of me. It wasn't a real long fall. It was early in the morning and it was kind of dark, but I could see him tumble. It was one of those times where I was so surprised; I couldn't imagine he was hurt. I was saying, "Are you okay," and those sorts of things.

All of a sudden he rolled over and he just screamed in pain—scared the living shit out of me. All of a sudden, bam! Holy cow, he's hurt. That kind of ties in, that first time you see your dad cry, the first time you see him hurt. And I was the only one there. I remember him having major pain. He hurt his leg. It looked like he almost came down on his neck. But he actually caught his leg kind of weird. Compound fracture, busted through, and I had to go and get help. I had to run about a mile up the trail to get some people that we knew that were hunting with us. We had to call an ambulance to get him in. Later on, I could see the blood actually coming through his snowmobile suit, that's how bad he was bleeding.

That image sticks in my mind, of him being hurt. It was one of the first times that I saw that he could be hurt. That really sticks in my mind. And then the time afterwards where he had to go through rehab. He was in traction for six months; he was out of work. It was real tough on the family because not a whole lot of money was coming in. He was at home for a good chunk of the time due to the heavy medication. It's just very weird to see your father in that sort of state, going through that sort of rehab, having multiple surgeries.

His femur exploded into eighteen different pieces and busted through, so they had to do a total reconstruction of everything. It's something that is really vivid in my head. That injury really caught me off guard and has always stuck with me—just seeing his vulnerability and him counting on us to take care of him. That was a pretty big wake up about life.

*10. What single trait or characteristic should all fathers own?*

Number one would be the son or daughter has got to think that they can depend on him. He doesn't have to be the greatest dad in the world. He doesn't have to do all those little things that supposedly make great dads, but when it comes down to crunch time, you have to be able to think, "My dad's there." I think that would be a huge one. Obviously Dad has made tons of mistakes like everyone does, but I think when it comes down to it, you've got to always feel like you can count on your dad..

The role model thing would just be huge. I don't want to sound like Old Man River, but I don't think a lot of dads today realize how big a role model they are, even when they don't think they are. The kids are at school. They're away somewhere with their friends. They're immersed in mass media twenty-four hours a day. I see dads that just say, "Whup, oh well." And those kids get their influences and role models from outside their home.

Those dads don't realize, they're still there. Be a role model, even in simple things. You don't have to be super dad, just show honesty, show dependability. Take care of business. That's pretty huge. I think too many parents are too easily relinquishing that role; they are almost willing to give it up. It's a lot of work, obviously. But being in school, I see that so often it just kills me. They just sort of wash their hands of it and, oh my God.

Just to tag on with those two things, I think my dad did a really good job with that. The whole role model thing and the dependability—as much as he frustrates the hell out of me sometimes, I always feel like when it comes down to it, he'd be there for me and I could always make that phone call.

# CHAPTER 5

# Carl

*1. What is your interview name and your real age?*

Carl, and I'm fifty.

*2. By what name do you call your father, Dad, Papa, and how did you arrive at that name?*

Dad. I called him Dad because that's what they told me to call him.

*3. How would people describe your father?*

Funny. Hard working. Probably sensitive.

*Do you agree with that?*

Yeah.

*4. Tell a story of your father teaching you a skill.*

We were going to retile the kitchen floor. And we weren't real sure how to get the old tile off the floor. So my dad went and got some dry ice and put it on the floor tiles; what it did was froze them. And all we had to do was take a putty knife and pop a corner, and the whole tile came up. Then all we had to do is clean the glue off the floor. I thought that was pretty cool.

And then he showed us how to lay the tile. You find the center point in a room and you measure off and all that stuff and you make lines before you just start throwing things down.

*5. Share an incident you experienced when you were proud of your father.*

This is a good one. It was Halloween. In earlier times, when the town was smaller, and we were in grade school, Halloween was a big thing. And it still is.

We went out for Halloween and came home. And we had some neighbors that lived a couple doors away; it was a mom and her daughter. We never saw the dad, so we assumed they didn't have one. And they didn't talk too much. But they had a big, old Aleppo pine tree that dropped a whole bunch of needles on their roof.

So we're sitting in our house. The way the house faced, we could see right down the street and see this other house. We saw the neighbor guys that were older than us in high school, come running around the corner, and then they were lighting newspaper and throwing it up on these people's roof.

So we're all checking it out and my dad says, "Do you boys know who those guys are?"

And I said, "Yeah, I know who they are." And I told him where they lived. So my dad ran down the street and chased them and walked right in their front door after them and told their dad what happened.

So, I was very proud of him then. I thought that was super cool. It was a brave thing to do because those guys were all athletes and we could have had retaliation, too. (Laughs.)

*6. Tell something you picked up or got from your father.*

Being thrifty with money. (Laughs.) I'd say sense of humor and thriftiness.

*7. Tell a favorite story about your dad.*

When I was learning to play guitar there was a Gretsch guitar that I wanted to buy. And I asked my dad to go down and pick it up for me at this music store. I was in high school and you know how you're all amped up and all that; so when I got home, it wasn't on my bed. And so I flipped out. I did. I flipped out.

My mom got really pissed off, giving me crap, how ungrateful I was and all that, because they went and got the guitar but they hid it. So they were messing with me. But when I got pissed off, then they chewed me out even more for being upset.

And I guess the moral of the story is just because you ask somebody to do something for you, they may not be able to do it. And if they can't, you shouldn't get pissed off.

My moral of the story is: If there's something that you're buying, go pick it up yourself. (Laughs.) That one sticks out. It was my first electric guitar.

Another one that sticks out, my dad used to shoot black powder canons. So we used to go out to the Buffalo Barbecue east of town; that was fun. He'd take us with him and they'd dress up in buckskins and shoot flintlock rifles and all that hoopla.

My friends used to get a big kick out of it, because sometimes we'd go out on the weekends. Some people would go fishing or golfing, my dad would load this canon up in his trailer or pull it with the Volkswagen bus, and we'd all hop in and take off to the desert—where of course it's all houses now. And we'd shoot that thing. (Laughs.) He'd shoot it at things like cars that had been abandoned, dirt embankments, and stuff like that. He was always real safe with it. He wasn't like, shoot it and see how far it would go. (Laughs.) No, he was always real safe. If it had been just us boys, it might have been a different story. He probably knew better.

I guess when his brother and he were growing up, they lived on a farm in Michigan, he bought an old signal can at an auction; they were going to shoot it on the Fourth of July. So they stuffed it full of gunpowder and wadded up paper and stuff, and it didn't go off. After about fifteen minutes, my uncle went out there and he was sticking his face in front of it, looking. He pulled his head back, and then vavoomph, it went off. (Laughs.)

8. *What's something you discovered later in life about your father that surprised you?*

Hmm. (Laughs.) I don't think there were many surprises; I pretty much knew what my dad was all about and all that stuff.

I would say it had to be the rest of my brothers working for each other. And then the way my dad took sides with the brother that basically, shafted (Laughs), everybody else. It didn't work out too well. The way my dad took sides with him, that surprised me. I thought he and my mom would have been more neutral, but they weren't. So that surprised me.

*9. Describe a particularly clear memory of being with your father.*

I have a couple particularly clear memories. I would say the times that he went on Boy Scout outings with us, and I also remember that sometimes he used to take us out. I don't know, because my mom got whacked out and he had to split or maybe we drove her nuts, and she said, "Get them the hell out of here."

He'd take us up to the corner Rexall and we'd go to the ice cream fountain and have whatever we wanted. I remember that. And also, sometimes we would go to a movie, maybe me and him and one of my other brothers. That didn't happen real often, but those are things that I remember.

*10. What single trait or characteristic should all fathers own?*

Patience. That would take care of it for me. (Laughs.) Patience. And refrain from laying guilt trips. (Laughs.) And don't be secretive or hold things in if they want to scold or reprimand. Just lay it out on the table. Don't avoid issues. You know what Winston Churchill said, "An issue avoided is a crisis created."

# CHAPTER 6

# Kenneth

*1. What is your interview name and your real age?*

Kenneth, and I'm thirty-two.

*2. By what name do you call your father, Dad, Papa, and how did you arrive at that name?*

Dad. Dad, Mom, we had a pretty close relationship. I think Pop would have been someone who's a little older. I think that it was important growing up. Dad was a younger father, so Papa kind of seemed like someone that would have been an older father. My dad was twenty-three when he had me.

*3. How would people describe your father?*

My dad is someone that many people would consider very giving, and very kind. Fun to be around, he's very fun loving. He's a very small person. He's five foot six and the life of the party; he always has a joke. People that knew him liked to be around him. He's a very generous man.

*And you agree with that?*

I do. I do. I mean they didn't see some of the same sides that I saw of him, because, of course, I was his son. They didn't see some of the things he'd been lacking, because usually people put their best foot forward in public.

When I was twelve I was taller than my dad. We had our differences. He was a military man and he expected certain things to happen.

*4. Tell a story of your father teaching you a skill.*

I don't think that my dad really was a hands on type of person. He didn't really teach me a lot of skills. My dad didn't come out and play baseball with me or participate in sports. Like I said, he was a very small man.

I think the thing he taught me most was people skills, maybe how to be respectful to women. And when you say you're going to do something, you should live up to that. Social skills might be more of what he taught me, rather than how to work on a car, or how to do these other types of things that most fathers would teach their boys.

And my dad's one of those people who gets along with pretty much anybody. And he can get through, even if he has a tough boss to deal with. People respect him because he's willing to go the extra to get along with other people. My dad's only fifty-six, so he's around.

*5. Share an incident you experienced when you were proud of your father.*

Every time that we have any kind of conflict in the United States, my dad was in the military. My father has received numerous military awards and I've always been very proud of him.

I remember in church, when he was put in a position of authority. I was very pleased and very honored that he was my father and that people would think enough of him to have him do that job.

When he was in Boy Scouts as one of the regional leaders, he helped lots of boys besides just my group of boys. I was very pleased then and proud of him. There have been a number of times when my dad's made me proud and made me look up to him a little bit, maybe not in stature, but in other ways.

*6. Tell something you picked up or got from your father.*

I think I have a pretty good sense of humor and I think that my dad probably taught me that. You always hear people say that you're going to hear yourself say what your father said in the way you discipline your kids, or the way you talk to your children. And that's so true. You know, not that my dad was always the best at disciplining. But, sometimes I do hear myself say some of the things my dad would say.

Sometimes, I reflect back, and see some of his mannerisms or things he did or said. Even though I'm a lot bigger than he is, I still have some of those same characteristics. I think I also have the same kind of voice tone that my dad has. My dad's a great singer; I love to sing, too. His voice is a little bit higher than mine, but we still have that same voice tone when we sing.

*7. Tell a favorite story about your dad.*

I've had some pretty crazy adventures with my dad. Probably the most fun I've had with him was when we'd go fishing in Oregon where I grew up. When I was twelve and thirteen years old, it was really important to me that we would spend that time together. And it was kind of like the only thing that we really had in common. I loved athletics; he did not. He was very busy. So, when we went fishing together, that was probably the time that we would bond the most and enjoy each other's company the most.

*8. What's something you discovered later in life about your father that surprised you?*

I don't think my dad held much to the vest, honestly. He just lays it out. Either you like him or you don't. Of course, every family has skeletons in the closet, but I know that he had a very, very difficult childhood. But I knew that growing up. My grandparents have been married three times together, and weren't married when I was born. My grandmother was married six times, and dad was the oldest child of four and his youngest brother died when he was a child, run over by a cement truck. So I knew quite a bit about him and some of the things he's gone through. I think, even with his hobbies and all these types of things, he's pretty well laid it out. I don't know, there aren't a lot of surprises that my dad gives me at this point. (Laughs.)

*9. Describe a particularly clear memory of being with your father.*

I remember carrying my dad out of a canyon one time. (Laughs.) He was either having a heart attack or a stroke of some kind, but some kind of physical malady. He couldn't walk, he was having labored breathing; it was hot out. It could have been heat stroke, but we're still not really sure.

I had to haul him out of a canyon. It seemed like about a mile deep. It really wasn't that bad, but I was fourteen years old. But because I was a big kid, and because Dad wasn't too big, it wasn't too big of a problem. I was close to six foot by fourteen and a half. It was one of those things. I remember at that age, you have a little turmoil with dad, that little challenge thing. You tell yourself, "Hey, am I man enough to handle him, yet? Can I take him?" You know how kids are.

And I think it was kind of an awakening for me, realizing how much concern and love I really did have for him, even with all the turmoil at home. Because he was to the point where I thought, "He's gonna die on me here." I came to the conclusion of how much I really would miss him and how much I did care for him, even though as a teenager, I usually was concerned about myself.

*10. What single trait or characteristic should all fathers own?*

I think a sense of obligation and responsibility to your children and to your wife, and then of respect and love. I really do believe that in this world we live in today, a lot of our problems come from a father not taking on responsibilities that he should live up to, teaching children the right things in life. The argument could be, what are the right things in life? But I can tell you that my dad didn't give me athletic skill or a desire for baseball or football or any of the other things I was very interested in. He may not have even given me a great drive for academia, but my father did teach me that sense of obligation and responsibility. I never heard my father be disrespectful to my mom, not that they never argued or anything like that. My dad always lived up to his obligations. He always paid his bills on time. Those were things that were very important to him. And I think that's probably growing up in the family that he grew up with too; farmers in the Midwest felt that those things were the most important.

I truly believe that just teaching our children responsibility, and how to live up to those commitments that we should be making, is something a father should do.

# CHAPTER 7

# Lee H.

## *Twin Brother of Scruggs*

*1. What is your interview name and your real age?*

My interview name is Lee H. My age is forty-one.

*2. By what name do you call your father, Dad, Papa, and how did you arrive at that name?*

Dad, that's the way I was raised. He was the daddy. He was the provider.

*3. How would people describe your father?*

Kind, I want to say sincere. What is the word I am looking for? Sensitive.

*Do you agree?*

In some ways he is. He's tough too, you know. Yeah.

*4. Tell a story of your father teaching you a skill.*

Hmmm, you got me thinking back. Driving a car. (Laughs.) It is kind of funny. I was getting old enough to drive. He said, "Oh Boy, I guess that time is coming."

He made me nervous too. And you don't want to make the driver nervous. But, he was okay at that. I guess he gave us the basics but driver's education did the rest.

And I was scared to drive with him, too. I was like, "That's okay. I'm not asking you any more."

5. *Share an incident you experienced when you were proud of your father.*

There's a lot. I guess when my daughter was born. He was just talking to me about how life is going to change tremendously, but not in a bad way. I can't remember all the things he said. But, I was of proud of him talking to me like that, because you know, no book comes on parenthood.

The proudest thing that really comes to my heart happened when we were kids. We were driving down the street and Dad said, "How do you guys like that house?" We said it was nice. Two days later we pulled up in the driveway of that same house and Dad said, "You guys are all home."

6. *Tell something you picked up or got from your father.*

I would say manners, respecting others.

7. *Tell a favorite story about your dad.*

He was trying to teach us to fish. We were in Arkansas. I could never get the rod right. Every time I'd throw the thing back, I couldn't time it right, and it would fall behind me. He threw his line in, and he waited a little while, then he caught a snake instead of a fish. And he got some rocks and he was trying to hit the snake off the pole. And we were just laughing. I thought that was kind of funny. I remember that, just like it was yesterday.

8. *What's something you discovered later in life about your father that surprised you?*

You know, my dad is very sincere, not outgoing, and he's kind of shy. I've known him for forty-one years and he has been a good provider for the family. But he worked all the time too.

My dad always showed love. But lately he has shown that he really loved my mom, his wife.

*9. Describe a particularly clear memory of being with your father.*

We were riding in the car one day and I was taking him to the doctor. My father's a diabetic. He just started crying for no reason, and I asked him what was the matter.

He said, "Getting old is no fun." I asked him why. He said, "If I could change the way that I took care of myself, I would."

*10. What single trait should all fathers own?*

They should be a good provider for their family. Their strength should be love, which fathers do, but not all of them. That's one thing Dad taught us—respect. And he hated it when we fought with each other. Oh, he did not like that.

"You all want to fight, fight me!" Oh he hated that with a passion.

And when we got into it, we couldn't go tell on each other, "What are you going to go tell for, you'll get a whipping." So we had to keep it amongst us. You know, four boys in the house. I sit back and think about that sometimes. And I think, "Man, that was something else."

# CHAPTER 8

# Scruggs

## *Twin Brother of Lee H.*

*1. What is your interview name and your real age?*

Scruggs, age forty-one.

*2. By what name do you call your father, Dad, Papa, and how did you arrive at that name?*

I call him Daddy, just born and raised saying that, and out of respect.

*3. How would people describe your father?*

Free hearted, warm, nice, respectful, happy.

*Do you agree?*

Oh, yeah, a hundred percent.

*4. Tell a story of your father teaching you a skill.*

He taught us how to get along with people and each other, and basically to love people.

*5. Share an incident you experienced when you were proud of your father.*

When I graduated out of high school he was proud of me. I was one of the first sons that graduated.

*6. Tell something you picked up or got from your father.*

I have to go back again to respect. The number one thing in our household was respect your elders and respect each other. I mean, he drilled that in us. If I see an old Black lady or an old White person or a Mexican person, I open the door for them. It is just how I am.

I say respect.

*7. Tell a favorite story about your dad.*

My dad was a good provider. He worked hard. He used to buy his four boys brand new bicycles every summer. And then we would hand down our old bikes to our cousins. Every year we got a brand new bike. I specifically remember the time when we were in the seventh grade.

*8. What's something you discovered later in life about your father that surprised you?*

Our dad spoiled us. He spoiled us. He never wanted us to do anything for ourselves—he always wanted to do it. And then when we got older, we didn't even know how to change the oil in the car.

My cousins were teasing us because we got new bikes every summer. While dad was buying us bikes, my first cousins were under the hoods of cars. We were living in luxury. While their mom and dad bought them hand-me-downs, we were going to JC Penney's and Sears and Dad was buying us clothes. I am not bragging on that, but that's basically what he did. It was like, "I can do this for my boys. I do this for my boys. They don't have to do this."

My momma said, "You are just spoiling those boys." And then when we got older, we didn't know what to do.

*9. Describe a particularly clear memory of being with your father.*

When my dad told me he was a diabetic. That kind of surprised me.

*10. What single trait or characteristic should all fathers own?*

A father must be a provider for his kids, teach them right and wrong, and teach them how to love.

Just be there for them, no matter what. Unconditionally.

# Chapter 9

# Leonard

*1. What is your interview name and your real age?*

My name's Leonard and I'm fifty-eight.

*2. By what name do you call your father, Dad, Papa, and how did you arrive at that name?*

Pop. And I don't remember why. I called him that ever since I was a kid. Pop. My mom called her dad, Pop. So I just called him Pop.

*3. How would people describe your father?*

Easy going. Laid Back. Real laid back. Mom was more or less the man of the house. He just sat back and let her take care of stuff. Laid back, I would say. Everybody I talked to saw him that way.

*Do you agree with that?*

No. Man of the house, being laid back, no.

*4. Tell a story of your father teaching you a skill.*

Driving, probably the first thing. He was a tough teacher, because he was a truck driver and everything had to be just right, just perfect. No mistakes. Because you couldn't make a mistake driving a truck or you were in trouble. I think he taught me to drive with a trucker's instinct. I guess it worked.

*5. Share an incident you experienced when you were proud of your father.*

Growing up, I was always real proud of everything about him. He wasn't a father that played ball and stuff with me. He was too wrapped up in other things.

The way he treated me after I first came back from Vietnam, with so much respect. The other stuff was kid's stuff from when I was little. And then the way he treated me when I returned from Vietnam after I'd been wounded; he treated me like a man, not a kid. He showed me a lot of respect, that more than anything.

It was different from when I went over. After I'd come back, we were friends, more than father and son. We were buddies. We hung around together. We'd go out together, we played pool together. We became buddies—more than father and son. I had grown up. I wasn't a kid any more.

*6. Tell something you picked up or got from your father.*

His habits, a lot of eating habits. Likes and dislikes. And respect for women. You never, under any circumstances, ever strike a woman. These are a couple things he really instilled in me. You respect a woman. If you get in an argument with your spouse, or your girlfriend, there's other ways to handle it. You don't go slapping them around or start screaming and yelling. I'm real laid back in that respect, and I got that all from him.

*7. Tell a favorite story about your dad.*

He bought my first car. My dad got my first car for me when I was sixteen like everybody gets a car when they are sixteen, more so now. But he bought this old car. An old farmer had it, and it was beat up and rusted out and everything.

He took that thing and put it in the garage and worked on it for about four months in all his spare time—filled in all the bad spots, replaced metal, sanded it, got it ready, and painted it. And then he gave it to me when it was ready. And that was my first car. That car meant more to me than any other I've ever had because of all the time and energy he put into it; he wanted to do that for me.

It was insurance money. I'd been in a car-bicycle wreck when I was nine, and they had put the money away. At that time it was only three hundred dollars, but that money stayed in there for me. He used that money to get that car and fix it all up. Like I say, I thought more of that car than any car I ever had.

*8. What's something you discovered later in life about your father that surprised you?*

After he passed away, my mom told me that she was the main person in the house. I never knew that until she told me; I always thought it was him. But later on I found out from mom that she pretty much had to initiate everything. Anything we ever had was mostly because of Mom. Like I said, he used to sit back and let her do things.

And as funny as it is, I'm just the opposite; a man is supposed to be in charge of his home. You're supposed to provide for your family. I don't hold it against him because he wasn't that way. I didn't know some of that stuff until after he passed away and I talked to mom. She said stuff that has stuck in my mind since.

*9. Describe a particularly clear memory of being with your father.*

After I got out of the service, we used to try to spend one weekend a month, just him and me. We'd go up to Bartlett Lake or something. Fish. Camp. Just the two of us. He always did all the cooking and I got to wash all the dishes. (Laughs.) That was something that he wanted to have, that time for just him and me. So I allowed that time too, him and me, one weekend a month.

During the good parts of the year, we'd go up, just the two of us, nobody else—back then you didn't have cell phones. But I allowed that. Just him and me, spending time together. I enjoyed his company.

*10. What single trait or characteristic should all fathers own?*

You have to be a kid's crutch and strength during their formative years and during their young adult years. You need to be there for your kids. Growing from a kid into a good adult isn't something that happens automatically.

The best thing a father can do is to be there for his kids during their formative and young adult years. Help them out—don't give them everything—but help them out. If they don't have somebody, they're missing out; growing up in today's world is even tougher than ours was. Thank God I had somebody there for me.

That's right. Fathers need to be there for their kids.

# CHAPTER 10

# Doug

*1. What is your interview name and your real age?*

My interview name will be Doug. My age is forty-seven.

*2. By what name do you call your father, Dad, Papa, and how did you arrive at that name?*

I call him Dad, because for the longest time, through high school even, I called him Daddy. He was Daddy. And then in college and early adulthood, it felt weird to say daddy. For years I just referred to him with my brother, and never really called him anything. And then I started calling him Dad. For a while it was really kind of awkward changing from daddy to dad.

*3. How would people describe your father?*

In many words, or in few words? My dad's a retired college professor now. I think they would describe him as a very kind, considerate man—almost the epitome of genteel. He's a very nice, very concerned, caring educator.

*Do you agree?*

Yeah. That's how I describe him and I think I'm pretty tied in with the mainstream.

*4. Tell a story of your father teaching you a skill.*

(Laughs.) A skill. I have a couple of them. One I'm going to have to tell too, because it's a funny story; the birds and the bees story.

I remember him teaching me how to throw a baseball. That's the stereotypic father teaching thing. And he had this old four-fingered glove. It was old. I'm sure he still has it. And he bought me a glove. Showed me how to put the ball in it and keep it oiled and everything. We did that and then played catch.

He taught me how to throw, "Put your left foot forward. Throw this way." I remember doing that in North Carolina. It was a back yard surrounded by trees, almost a canopy of trees over us in the yard. I still have images of that.

Also in that same yard, I remember him telling me the facts of life; the birds and the bees story. I don't remember much of it, but I do remember he used the word, fits. (Laughs.) The penis fits in the vagina—like a bolt in a certain size hole. (Laughs.) Only this nut fits with this bolt—it was very technical. It was obviously hard for him to tell that to his oldest kid.

*5. Share an incident you experienced when you were proud of your father.*

I remember one time, when he was getting his Doctor's degree, his PhD. I was little; I was in second grade. And we went to the ceremony and it was pomp and circumstance. It seemed regal to me. It was at Florida State University, so they went through a lot of different things and when they got his grad school, they did the hooding. It was pretty cool. That was a proud moment.

Other times are when he's talked about. I've taught in the same state he's taught in, and I've met some of his students. They say, "You're Mr. Doug's son! You're related to him?" And then tell me stories.

Or kids would come to me and say, " Oh, I had your dad down at the university." It's a special source of pride to know that we taught the same kids.

*6. Tell something you picked up or got from your father.*

My passion and enthusiasm for teaching other people. Both my parents were teachers at different ends of the age spectrum. My mom was a kindergarten teacher and my dad taught college. And they both loved it. They still do. They still love teaching people. They go on cruises and elder hostels and all kinds of stuff and just share their knowledge all the time with people (Laughs.) And I do that.

When I see kids at the park looking at a bird, I'll tell them, "He's this and you can see him catch a fish," and all this other stuff. I think that's probably the main thing I picked up from him. Maybe a love for music, too. I listened to a lot of Herb Alpert and the Tijuana Brass, musicals, Andy Williams, and Glen Campbell. My dad's Easter tradition is to play *Jesus Christ Superstar*, every year, cover to cover, all four sides.

*7. Tell a favorite story about your dad.*

(Laughs.) We went through a father/son YMCA camp; some kids in the neighborhood and the dads and just friends all got together. It was a father/son camp at a YMCA on a beautiful lake about an hour and a half from our house in northern Wisconsin. I don't know what the schedule was, but one of the activities was an activity similar to capture the flag; it was like a war game. This was in the days before paintball. We had little squares of toilet paper that you'd put a dollop of flour or baby powder in, tie the corners up with a rubber band, and you had yourself a missile that you could throw. And if you hit somebody and they had powder on them, they're done and they had to go to the tent. It was night and it was great. It was sons against the dads and my brother and I were running through the woods. Right at evening time is a great time.

My dad recanted the story afterwards; that's how we found out about it. He and some other dads got powdered, so they were out of the game, but they decided to come back from the dead (Laughs) and just scare kids.

So they went out and they threw some powder at some kids

and the kids turned and yelled, "Dads!" And they just started chasing them and my dad started running down this firebreak at full speed. Being evening time, he didn't see the chain stretched across the road about chest high (Laughs.) And boom, he hit the chain, flipped under, and landed flat on his back and couldn't catch his breath. And when he did start to breathe a little bit, there were all (Laughs) these little kids pelting him with powder and all these toilet paper squares and flour. He had a big chain link welt across his chest for weeks after that.

There are several lucky stories about my dad such as falling off a ladder onto his back from about eight feet onto the concrete. Yep. He also fell off a horse once on a trail ride in New Mexico. The horse galloped, he lost control, and the horse stopped and then threw him. He heard this loud, loud noise, this loud crack like a ball peen hammer on a four by four. Then he realized that was his head hitting a rock. (Laughs.) You know, he's survived some weird things.

*8. What's something you discovered later in life about your father that surprised you?*

Sharing his college exploits with me. Funny college stories we shared after I went to college and while I was in college—because he was a college Professor, a PhD. I heard stories of him taking a cow into the administration building, leading the cow up the stairs at night, and locking him in. (Laughs.) It's almost *Animal House* thirty years before *Animal House* came out. (Laughs.)

*9. Describe a particularly clear memory of being with your father.*

Since both my parents were educators, we had summers off and we'd travel. And we'd travel cheap—camping, tent camping, and tent trailer camping. So I have trip memories of him, driving and never letting my mom drive. Just constantly driving long distances. You know, got to make good time. And we went, "All right, today we went eight hundred miles."

We were driving to get places, but still stopping. His driving wasn't that driven, because we'd play all kinds of games in the car and read. We spent a lot of time traveling. So that's one of my major memories of time spent with him.

Later, going on trips with the family and with my son, even meant traveling in European countries where they drive on the wrong side of the road. Even then, Dad drove, which was good, because I don't think I could switch my brain that way.

Now that my son's older he says, "We have to go over to Ireland again. We have to go again." That was one of the favorite times in my life—my brother, my son, and my parents over in Ireland traveling around. Dad was driving this cheap little car they bought because they were there for a long time. The five of us were stuffed in that cheap little car. And every time we'd hit any kind of bump, it would sound and feel like it hit bottom as the suspension grated against the ground.

My mom would say, "Hunhh?"

And my dad would just reply, "Arrr."

*10. What single trait or characteristic should all fathers own?*

Kindness. I think they should be kind. Gentle kindness is a huge strength. It doesn't seem like it is, but it doesn't even have to be a firm gentle, kindness. It can just be gentle kindness. I don't think kids appreciate kindness as strength until they are in the position of being a father.

# Chapter 11 *

# Neb

* The ten questions are listed as numbers only after the first ten Chapters.

*1.* Neb, and fifty-nine.

*2.* Pop. I have no idea how I arrived at that name. It was basically something that I started using. I just called him Pop because it was short and sweet.

*3.* I think people would describe my father as a very quiet, caring man. They would describe my dad as a traditional Hispanic, family man. They would describe him as a man of strong family values who cared very much for my mother and worked hard to provide the entire family with a decent life.

I agree with those.

*4.* (Laughs.) You have to understand that my dad was a laborer for Kennecott Copper Corporation. He was a carpenter/handyman. He did a lot of manual jobs in the beginning—digging ditches, filling the ditches, et cetera. He did a lot of work with shovels. And then later on in his life he became a carpenter.

A Skill. A simple skill is how to use a shovel correctly. I remember that I was helping him mix some cement, pour the cement, and do a rock wall around the house. And so I (Laughs) took the shovel and started shoveling sand. Basically it was a disaster because of course; I was getting the sand all over the place.

So he said, "Stop. You're working too hard. This is how you handle a shovel." He quickly took the shovel and said, "If you are right handed, you put it over in your right hand and use your left foot. And when you take the sand, or whatever it is that you're shoveling, you want to put it directly in that spot. And this is how you do it." So he took the shovel and started doing the shoveling. Amazingly enough the sand came off the shovel in one clump and landed exactly in the spot that he wanted. So it took me maybe five or ten minutes of doing it when I finally realized, yeah, I was working too hard; I needed to work more efficiently, and learned the technique of how to use a shovel. It came in handy doing projects around the house, whenever I worked with a shovel. I was laying some cement the other day, and whenever I am working with a shovel, I always remember my dad teaching me that very simple task of doing it correctly.

5. Gosh, there's so many. There are so many. In his failure to do something, I was proud of him for trying and attempting it. My father was a carpenter/handyman for the Kennecott Copper Corporation. And in order for him to go ahead and become a carpenter, he had to pass a written test in math. My father didn't have much schooling; he was out helping the family of nine brothers and sisters at an early age. And my grandfather moved around quite a bit, pretty nomadic, spent most of the time in southwestern Arizona, going from towns like Mammoth to Hayden, Winkleman to Globe and Miami—never staying very much in one place. In fact, early on, he came to Phoenix and worked the fields. My dad also worked at the Dolan Box Factory; it was an old, old company way back then and doesn't exist any more. So Dad never had the opportunity to go to school very much.

So after working with Kennecott for several years, I'd say maybe twenty years, he got the opportunity to increase in rate and title from a carpenter/handyman to a carpenter. He had to take a math test in order to qualify, so he came to me and asked me to tutor him in math to help him out. And I said, "Okay. I will try." And of course, not being (Laughs) the best math student myself, we both struggled.

Needless to say, my dad did not pass the test.

When he finally told us that he had not passed the test and would not become a carpenter, I knew that he was very sad, very disappointed. And you could tell that in my father because he very much wanted to do that. It was a goal in his life that he wanted to accomplish, but he never accomplished it.

And it was a sad time because I knew, I could see, that it really did affect him quite a bit, that his lack of education kept him back. And in spite of that, my father continued to work with the company for another twenty-seven years as a carpenter/handyman. His buddies that passed the test became carpenters and he was their assistant. Needless to say, his skills were no less than his friends, but yet he did not have the title. I always was proud of him for having attempted it, for overcoming that stigma, and for overcoming that failure, because he continued on and worked and slaved for us, for Mom, for another twenty-seven years. I was always very proud. In spite of his failure, it was pretty touching.

6. Several things, I would have to say my father was a very quiet man. I think a lot of it was because he was not very sure of himself, as far as English was concerned. He spoke English, but not very well. He was a very quiet and reserved man.

He was one that judged people very well. He always stood back and was reserved. And I think I got a lot of that. I think I got the ability to sit back, look at the situation and the people, assess it all, and to really know who my friends are. That's one.

I think more so is his love for his family, his children—more than anything else. He always treated us as equals and his attitude was basically, "You have to learn for yourself. But yet, I'm always going to be here. Right or wrong, I'm still here."

That sense of judgment of his children is something that I carried to mine, in the sense that I was always behind my kids, whatever they did, right or wrong. But I let them try first and do things, regardless if they made a mistake or not. I always tell my kids, "I'm here. I'll be here."

He loved his grandchildren. How he loved his grandchildren; and watching how he … (Trails off, unfinished).

7. Oh gosh. There's so many of them. One stands out, one time. As I said, he loved his grandkids, and always got so excited when he had the opportunity to spend time with them. When Jennifer, my daughter, was born, he would always find any excuse to come down and spend time with his grandkid. Jennifer was still in a little baby carriage, so she had to have been seven, eight months along; she wasn't even in the crawling stage. And he came by one time on a weekend, and spent some time with us.

He came down by himself; he drove his Volkswagen. When it was time for him to go back home, I had already asked Jennifer's mother, "Think it's okay if Dad takes Jennifer and she spends the week with Mom and Dad?" And she said sure; Jennifer was old enough.

So I went over to my dad, once he was leaving, and said, "Hey Pop. You want to take Jennifer with you?"

And without hesitation he just lit up and said, "Yeah. Sure!" What a sight, him taking off in the Volkswagen with Jennifer in the little bucket seat there on the floor of the passenger's side of the Volkswagen. When he got home to Hayden, and parked the Volkswagen there by the house, Mom came out and said glad you're back and the greetings, and my dad said, "I got something for you."

She said, "What?"

So he said, "Come here." And she went out and looked in the front seat and there was Jennifer, just smiling away.

And mom said, "Oh my God. You did this all by yourself, you managed to bring her?"

He said, "Yeah."

Mom asked him, "Was there any problem, was she crying?"

"No. I sang to her all the way."

It's a cool story. It's just his attitude; he had it with all of his grandchildren.

*8.* There weren't too many things that were surprising about Dad.

Well, here's a good one. When I was in high school, this is a good example of my father, somehow we got on a conversation about prejudice. My high school was about fifty-fifty in regards to Hispanic and Anglos, and I had been included in just about every aspect of high school life and stuff like that. But somehow we got into a conversation and I said, "There isn't any prejudice. I don't see any prejudice."

It was just a philosophical conversation, but then my dad got a little serious. And he said, "Wait a minute. Let me tell you something. You may not encounter it, you may not see it, but it's there. And you have to go into the world as an adult with your eyes open, with an open mind. It's there. You are going to encounter it. And you need to deal with it. How you deal with it, that's up to you."

So he told me a story. He had been on a road trip as a youngster in his late twenties, out in Texas. And he and some buddies stopped at a roadside diner, and they sat at the counter, and nobody came over to serve them. Everybody else was served, and so they waited there for fifteen, twenty minutes, and nobody came by. And they finally decided, okay, it's not going to happen. So they got up and they left. I never knew that my father had experienced that. And I say that in the sense that my dad was a gentle soul who was a good man who would not harm anyone. That he had experienced prejudice in that fashion was a surprise to me.

But yet, his relating that to me was not in the sense that he held a grudge—it was just that it happens. And so you need to understand that it happens. And you deal with it. I guess if I were in the same circumstances, I would either pound my fists on the counter and say, "I want some service!" or else just let it go and walk out. However, I think in those days, there wasn't much of a choice; you had to walk out.

*9.* Clear memories of being with my father, most definitely are fishing trips. Every summer, my brother who lives in Albuquerque, and his two children and myself and my three, would meet up in the Big Lake area of Greer in northeastern Arizona. We would do this three or four times a summer. We would spend four, five days every time up there. This was our routine; it was traditional. We would go. Every year. And my dad was never excluded from that. He always went.

My three kids and I would drive down to Hayden and pick up my dad. He always had a small, little duffel bag that he kept his stuff in, and then he would get in the truck in the front seat and we would take off. And it was something that when the kids were young, and they were always included, they always went—it was always the kids spending time talking to Dad and his interchange with his grandchildren. Rachel, my youngest daughter, was very, very close to him. My recollections of doing the road trip with my dad are my dad talking to the kids and the kids listening to him.

Rachel mimics him. She's the spitting image of my father. My father had these sayings, what we call Manuelismos, named after him. And a Manuelismos is like a saying that my dad invented. I'll give you two examples, "You betchem Red Ryder, you bet your boots in the morning." They are nonsensical sayings, what you might call a ghost whistle.

Every time I talk to my daughter Rachel, she still has these things internalized. And she'll respond in a greeting with my dad's sayings. She'll say goodbye with one of my dad's sayings. And it's the fishing trips, and the bonding there. The fishing trips that we went on, watching and listening to my dad interact with my kids.

Later on when my children and my brother's children grew up and moved out of the house to have their own careers and families, it was just the three of us—my brother, myself, and my dad. And on those trips, when I would pick up my dad to go fishing, we would drive for hours and hours without saying a word to each other. But just knowing that he was there, and having him there, I knew that he was enjoying the moment. He was enjoying the idea of going fishing, and sometimes I think that the reason for that was that he was remembering too, thinking of the grandkids.

But we would drive for hours and once in a while I would check and I'd go, "Hmm?"

And he'd go, "Ah." That was it. (Laughs.)
"Hmm?"
"Hmm." And we would stop and have something to eat.

It was those trips, with the kids first and then the three of us. The interesting thing about this is my father passed away in September ninety-eight, and my brother and I still get together in the summer time. I'm going to go in about three weeks with my bro up to Big Lake. We still get together and do some fishing.

About a year ago, my brother and I were sitting there beside the lake; we had our lines in, and we're sitting in these little chairs, and we hadn't spoken for about twenty minutes and we kind of just looked at each other and started laughing.

So I said to my brother, "So this is what it's come down to. It's just the two of us." And as a tradition when we go fishing, we set out a third chair, because dad's always there.

*10.* Have an open mind and be able to accept your children as they are. Give them the opportunity to become themselves because they will become their own individual person by watching the examples that a father or mother sets. I think it's a big imprint on the child. Patience and understanding and letting them grow up to be their own person. I know that my father was never in the forefront, always in the background. Yet, right or wrong, he was there.

# Chapter 12

# Leo

*1.* My name is Leo and I'm fifty-two.

*2.* My father left our family when I was about two-and-a-half. So I never called him anything.

*3.* Everybody to a person has described my father as a very personable, funny, outgoing, self-destructive man.

When I met him, the self-destruction of years of alcoholism had kind of overshadowed much of the rest of it. He was confined to a wheelchair, and he had very little energy. He realized, and had many regrets about his life. He realized that he had screwed up this chance. This was not a dress rehearsal.

*4.* (Laughs.) That would be tricky. I've got all these surrogate fathers I could tell you stories about.

I know that all my life I have been an avoider of arguments. And I swear that's because at the age of two, two-and-a-half, hearing my parents arguing had an effect on me. There's something visceral when I hear people argue; I just want to be away from it. I think it's environmental; I don't think it's genetic.

After my father left, it profoundly affected my brother, who was six—how kids feel it's their fault. It did not affect me, but what I began to notice at about the age of four and five was all these men hanging around. And it wasn't that they were trying to date my mother, it was that they were trying to help. My two uncles are both outdoorsmen; so I spent every weekend out in the desert or up fishing or mountain climbing because of them.

And two of our next-door neighbors and another neighbor down the street went to great lengths to try to father me. They went to scout meetings with me. They showed me how to mow yards. They took me under their wings. In fact, two of them had other children and that caused problems later on because they said their fathers liked me more than they liked them. (Laughs.) Which was because they had no real, hard-core responsibility for me; I'm sure it wasn't because I was more likable.

And so everywhere I looked, in fact, I had almost too many fathers. I remember for scout meetings that one of my surrogate fathers would take me one week, and the following week another one would take me; that caused great confusion for people that didn't really know what was going on.

Later, a number of my coaches also, when they realized my situation, somehow felt that they had to fill a gap. I was never aware that there was a gap. I just knew that these people—and now in retrospect, I have a great deal of respect for them—seemed to be always there and wanting me to do fun stuff with them.

5. Haven't got one. (Laughs.)

6. I think that I got a part of his personality, not that I'm particularly outgoing, but compared to the rest of my family, I am. My brother and my mom have very similar personalities. And I've always been a little on the odd, outside of that. I remember Mother always saying when I did something, "That was your father." And she saw all these little instances of things.

I think I got a lot of my behavior characteristics from him. I think that occasionally my father, who came over from Ireland when he was seventeen, had trouble with the truth. And I think there've been times in my life where I have too. (Laughs.)

There's a famous Irish line; "Is that the truth?"

The answer is almost always, " Well, that's about as close as you're going to get." And I know that I inherited some of that from my father, too.

I remember at two, the whiskers when he'd hold me up against his cheek. I remember that very clearly. My father, when he lived here, was a horse trainer at the racetrack. He was in Chicago, too. And so I remember the smell of horses and I remember going out to the track; we drove forever to get out to Turf Paradise. So I remember that fairly clearly.

I remember being a little guy and hearing the parties that went on in the house. There would be five or six couples in there. But when I got older, that didn't happen—my mother stayed very much to herself. But I remember those parties. From my crib I could hear that, and I thought they were wonderful. I love that sound of distant laughter and stuff. (Laughs.)

7. My father, because of his horse connections, knew a number of fairly famous athletes. So when my mother and father got married, Jack Dempsey and Joe Louis and Joe DiMaggio came to the wedding. My parents were not wealthy. And we do have a couple pictures here and there of these people at the wedding—oh, and a number of mob guys out of Chicago too, which is why my father had to leave Chicago. I just thought it was so cool that celebrities showed up to their wedding.

8. Boy, this is not going to be complementary. What surprised me is he was married and had children before he married my mother. And then he was married and had children and actually killed two of his children in a car wreck, after my mother. But I didn't know until social security records came, because when he got disability, we got some child support disability and it listed previous dependents of his. We all went, "He had a family before?" It was kind of a surprise.

9. He came and visited occasionally. I remember when I was five or six, my brother was eight or nine, and he came to visit; we lived in San Jose. He took us out for ice cream and we went to a

bookstore and bought books and went to The Toy Cottage and we each got to pick a toy. And we went home and he sat on the floor and played with us. And I remember when he got up to leave that he was crying. And I thought, why are you crying? But now I know. (Laughs.)

*10.* Patience. Patience. And by that I don't mean tolerating things, I mean not overtly showing disappointment in behavior that doesn't quite come up to par. I know too many kids who, whatever they did, their father had an attitude of, "That wasn't quite good enough." Or, "You should have done this." I've been on enough athletic teams in my life, where I remember seeing lots and lots of kids' dads doing that. And always being grateful that I didn't have, not necessarily even overt criticism, but that kind of covert father hanging his head when the kid did something bad in the field. And I knew that kids always noticed that in their fathers. I felt incredibly liberated from that. That was important.

So patience. That was a long answer. (Laughs.) The same patience that I would hope God shows to us. You know, we screw up. (We both laughed.) I hope he doesn't sit there and frown and scowl.

We were talking about dads being involved and being committed. I've often heard it described as being like bacon and eggs.

With the eggs, the chicken was involved. But with the bacon, the pig was committed.

# CHAPTER 13

# Tom

*1.* Tom. And I'm seventy-one years old.

*2.* I called him Pop. To me, it was easier to say.

*3.* My father was a very kind and gentle person. He worked hard all his life, but he never really got anywhere. I told him the only reason he never got anywhere was because he was too honest.
Yes I do.

*4.* We were born and raised on a farm on Seventy-ninth and Camelback, and our theme in those days was work and plenty of it. I was on a tractor at fourteen years old. I was hauling grain to the mill at fourteen years old. And I was milking cows at fourteen years old plus going to high school. That was the name of the game—it was work.
It was a hard life for him. It's not that way today at all, because the farms are gone. The cities are in now. It's a different environment now. Now it's get in the front of a TV and see how many hamburgers you can eat.

*5.* I was always proud of my father because he always stood up for me. I stuck up for my father because he never lied to nobody.
In our church, my grandfather was a preacher. Later on, my father was a preacher too in the same church. So I was proud of the

fact that my father took after his father. That was a proud moment in our lives, his too. Yeah, he was a preacher. That was pretty good.

6. I picked up his values like being truthful and honest about stuff, and not lying. Because that's how my father was. The values he gave me, I think they were great, because they're good to live by.

My conscience doesn't bother me about what I do because I know it's the truth. Those are the values that my father gave me.

7. My father farmed in Casa Grande for about ten years. He raised cotton over there from 1960 to 1970. When they went to church on Sundays, my mother and my father had to come to Glendale. They lived out on the farm over there.

And one time, there were some ants in the sink, and they were kind of rolling around in there, and they couldn't get out. So before my father left, he got a stick, and he put it in the sink to the top of the sink, so the ants could get out. (Laughs.) That's a true story.

My father had that kindness in him. Even to ants. Honest. It's true. Most people wouldn't do that. But my father did.

And here's a second story. When my brother and I went to high school, to keep tabs on us so we wouldn't wander off, my father bought some cows. So we milked them in the morning and in the evening. That went on for four years. And then after we graduated from high school, it was really something. All of a sudden, my father sold all the cows. And we didn't have to milk cows any more. (Laughs.)

8. The biggest surprise was when my father passed away. That was a shock to all of us because it wasn't through his health.

He had NH3 gas out in the field for the cotton. One time after the water stopped, when finished irrigating, instead of just turning the handle off, he smelled it to see if the gas was still running. And it knocked him down.

Eventually, it perforated his lungs. My father died from lung cancer, but my father never smoked a cigarette in his life. When my father passed away at seventy-two, it was a shock to all of us, the whole family. I wouldn't call it a surprise; it would be more like a shock.

NH3 gas is a fertilizer; it's a gas that you put in the water. Psst. It's like a fog when it comes out—like a steam. It goes in the water and when it hits your plants, it gives them nitrogen. It gives plants more strength to grow.

That's what he did. And he paid for it. A matter of fact, when he went in the house, he told my mother, "One of these days, I gonna pay for that." And he did.

9. I worked there with my father during the harvest of the cotton. I rode a cotton-picker for him. He had three cotton-pickers and I ran one of them for him during the cotton season. I still lived in Glendale, but I'd go home on the weekends.

He needed some guidance over there and I was there to help him out. He was there for ten years, from 1960 to 1970. Yeah, it was hard work.

10. A son has to believe in his father. He has to believe what he does, and what he thinks, and what he wants you to do. And that's the strength that you get from your father, from his strength. If you don't believe in your father, then you don't believe in much of anything.

Oh yeah. It's an everyday thing. It's like on the job training. Everyday you do it, and you learn something every day. And that goes on for the most of your life, too.

My father was believable. When he said something, it was true. It wasn't a joke. That's how he was.

He didn't joke around much, but I do. Where I picked that up, I don't know. I think it was the guys I ran around with when I was in school. I got some crazy uncles. (Laughs.) Yeah, I had an uncle that was a joker; well, a couple of them were as far as that goes.

# CHAPTER 14

# Chief

*1.* My name is Chief and I'm thirty-four.

*2.* I call him Dad, just call him Dad. I met my dad when I was about sixteen; I just called him Dad right off the bat. He was my biological father and that's who he is.

*3.* Boy, there are a lot of different ones there. My grandma hates him; well, she probably doesn't hate him as much now, but when he was younger, he was known as a womanizer, one of sixteen kids. (Laughs.) They're all halves.

But my dad now is known as a preacher. Now he's known as a good-hearted guy. Back when, he was a little different from what I hear. And I believe it too. I've seen him go after people for hurting my sister, and stuff like that. I've seen my dad crazy and I've seen him very peaceful. Very, very peaceful. (Laughs.)

He's an ordained minister and he can marry people and stuff like that. He's not all in the Book of God, always with God. Wherever you make your path in life, he encourages it.

My second youngest brother is right now over in Iraq in the Marines. He was there during the fall of Fallujah. And my dad, he's just scared. My dad is scared. I've never seen my dad really scared about any of the siblings except for him.

My brother kept telling my dad, "I want to go there to be a man. I want to go there to be a man." He didn't realize he can be a man just by being himself. Now it's changed.

*4.* Well he tried to teach me a skill when we lived in Texas for a while. He had his own restaurant and he tried to have me totally manage it. I was about sixteen, right after I met him. I went down there and worked there for a little while. When my dad would have to go do stuff, I would mind the whole store. We had pool tables and I ran pool tournaments, closed up shop. Plus, I also went to school and played football and stuff like that.

He has the gift for gab, my dad does, but I don't really have it. So I really couldn't learn anything like that. Like they say, he can sell ice water to an Eskimo; he's one of those types. He used to be a vacuum cleaner salesman for a vacuum cleaner company called Tri-Star, way back in the seventies. He used to buy them for a couple hundred dollars and go sell them for nine hundred to a thousand dollars, all the attachments and all that stuff. He was pretty good at it, I guess. And then he was a truck driver.

That's what I want to go back into now is truck driving. He's been talking to me about that. I've been driving most of my life already. I figure if I'm going to be driving, I might as well make some money and build my family like I want to now. I figure I've reached that age of maturity to where it's not like, "Yeah. Let's go party," every night. I want to stay home and relax.

*5.* I was up in Oregon about two years ago and my dad asked me to help him build a porch. And me and my dad never did anything like that, never did any kind of construction. My dad asked me for help.

It just made me proud of him that he wanted me there to come help him, wanted me there early to come have breakfast, and coffee. Just do all that stuff. Eat there at dinner time. While in the rain, put those little slats that go up so the rain can run off. My dad had back surgery so I did most of the hard work; he's real knowledgeable and stuff. So I was proud of him.

Plus, also the time he chased down the guy for hurting my sister. (Laughs.) That's almost a given for me.

But, I've been real proud of him for how he raised my two sisters and my brother. I'm real proud of him for that. My brother and sister, their mother died, got murdered in Texas, and he started raising them totally. He was in their life when they were real young and then when the divorce came through, there was a battle.

When she died, he took them in when they were nine and eleven and raised them right. My sister is bilingual in Spanish up in Oregon and she's doing her college stuff. I think he's done real well with us; sometimes he hasn't been around, but I think a lot of his personality carried down into us.

6. (Immediately.) I got an eye blink. I got a very bad eye blink. It seems to happen a lot of times when I get nervous. I'll be just sitting there, and usually both of them will start twitching real bad and start closing and opening and closing and blinking. That or it'll just be one eye will be doing it and going crazy. I've got a real bad eye tick, a real, real bad eye tick.

And it's just like his. I never knew he had it until one day I noticed that he was doing it. I've had that all my life. So I inherited it. (Laughs.)

7. I was in trouble when I was fifteen. They were going to send me to Adobe Mountain Boys Ranch, that or a foster home because my mom couldn't control me. I talked to my dad; that's when I first met him. I talked to him on the phone and I told what was going to happen. He said, "My son ain't going nowhere like that." And he came all the way to Arizona to take me back to Texas.

And he told the judge, "I know my rights; I've had kids in this state, and you're not putting my kid in Adobe Mountain. I will take him to Texas now." And that's what he did. We drove twenty-four hours to Henrietta, Texas.

When I first got there, he had a house. And then his wife wanted a divorce and all this stuff happened; so we had to go live at another place for a while. We kind of bounced around and I ended up at my friend James's house, and doing part of my junior year of high school there. I had scholarships lined up for football and everything. I played eight years of football; so I was really into it.

*8.* That he actually could get scared. (Laughs.) I'd never seen my dad scared until I listened to him talk on the telephone about my brother, and how he worries about him. Sometimes he tries to avoid the conversation of my brother, because it worries him, but I bring it up.

I'll say, "How is he? Have you heard from him? He doesn't talk to me." That's the only time I've seen him being scared.

*9.* Oh, Christmas. It was my first Christmas with my dad. I went up to Oregon. I never had Christmas with my dad, never been around my dad for my birthday either. And I went up there for Christmas.

It was the first time I was actually ever part of anything with my brothers and my sister, the first time I was ever there. And I had long, long hair and I have pictures of him and me together. It was pretty close, pretty nice, something I had never even experienced before.

*10.* Stern care with their kids. I think fathers and mothers, particularly fathers, have totally ventured away from their kids. They back away from their kids and I think that's wrong. I haven't seen my daughter in almost ten years. I wish my wife wasn't the way she is with me. I would love to see my daughter. I've tried. I've tried and I've tried.

But be stern. Be stern about your kids. You have to be. It's the only way they are going to be raised right, especially in this city, but all over too.

Like they say, we are raising leaders. Let's raise them right. Let's train them right. Let's show them, instead of all these political people messing up our whole system anyway.

# CHAPTER 15

# Jason

*Nephew of Alfred, John Henry, and Ralph*
*2ⁿᵈ Cousin of Richard*

*1.* Jason and I'm eighteen.

*2.* I usually call him Dad or Pops, because Poppa is overused all the time and I just thought of something original.

*3.* Upon first meeting him, he seems strict and scary. But after meeting him and getting to know him, he has a thick skin but he's a very nice guy.
Yes.

*4.* I remember going out to the shop as a young kid, and him having either a hot rod or some little project he was working on, from changing oil in the car to sawing a piece of wood and making it perfect.

*5.* Most recently I have been very proud of him after we finished the hot rod. When we would go to hot rod shows, such as Oklahoma City where he actually won Director's Pick for best car, you could see him smiling and being proud of the work that he did. Instead of what everybody else mainly does, which is have somebody else build the car for them, he did it all—except for paint and the interior.

6. (Quickly.) A sense of independence. He is a very independent man and has very great money management skills that I will probably never match but I hope to gain some of that from him.

7. After every high school football game, especially my senior year, we would be dog tired no matter whether we won or lost. Mom and Dad would always come over after the game and give us a hug.

If we were sad for losing, then they'd say, "It's okay, you have a new game next week." But, I would always notice my father's very limited smiling. And so, whenever you'd see him smile after a game of winning, it always put a smile on my face and I'd feel pretty good at that moment.

With our family, it's very hard to sit down and eat a meal together with everybody growing up and having their own schedules to deal with. But no matter, Christmas and Thanksgiving and Easter we would have a meal together, big or small, with the extended family that was around.

And my father got in the tradition of saying the prayer. And no matter what he said, be it in the beginning or in the end, he would add, "Always wish and hope that the food would nourish our bodies." It would make us chuckle, especially because over time, it became a custom that we would expect him to say it. "May this food nourish our bodies."

8. I guess with his formal education. I didn't cope, or I didn't understand for a while that he didn't go to college. He has quite a few skills in the mechanical area, but I guess that's something he's gained on his own.

But growing up as a kid myself, I was taught that most people do go to college and get an education, and my parents expect that of me.

*9.* As a kid, my Mother would be so busy with college work; we'd change it up in the family and every Sunday afternoon after church, my father and I would go to the store and spend an hour and a half, two hours doing our weekly grocery shopping together—pushing the cart and getting all the supplies necessary that we needed for that week. It was a regular thing every week.

*10.* I'm glad my father was not necessarily strict, but he taught me not to be hard headed. He wouldn't baby us, which was key, especially with growing up and going in the real world. He was very independent. I guess he had the right amount of being strict and the right amount of compassion, caring, and love for us kids, while not spoiling us. I'm glad for that, because it has made me grow up and feel more independent about myself, and to not rely on them fully—even though I am the youngest one and they consider me the spoiled one.

# CHAPTER 16

# Richard

*Cousin of Alfred, John Henry, and Ralph*
*2ⁿᵈ Cousin of Jason*

*1.* Richard, fifty-two.

*2.* Dad, that's just what I've always called him, just Dad.

*3.* Kind, gentle man, loved the outdoors, fishing, mostly. Just loved to be around family and friends.
Yeah, yeah.

*4.* Well, mechanical type work you know, as far as taking care of vehicles, that type of thing. That's a skill that you need to know today anyways. Changing oil, plugs; working on cars. And fishing, of course, he enjoyed that.

*5.* Going back a long ways, he mentioned to me one time that he turned down a position where he worked at the flourmill because supervisory positions would require more time away from the family than what he wanted to give. Today, I probably would have taken more money, but he didn't. That's something that I felt was a good thing that he did. I was proud of him for that.

*6.* I think that I got personality from him; he passed that along to me, hopefully. Otherwise I think I'm a kind person, and I have fond memories of going fishing and just doing outdoors types of things.

*7.* I remember one time we were at some friends' house—this is going back about thirty, forty years—and there was a storm that came by. This was in an old, farmhouse and we had to go in the cellar and Dad was keeping everybody calm and made my brother and I feel like we were safe. I was really scared until he said everything was going to be all right, and it was.

*8.* Just the other day my brother closed out a safety deposit box. He said, "Did you know that Dad had bought a patent with somebody else?"

I said, "No I didn't." So he hasn't come over yet to show me what it was. It's something that I didn't know anything at all about. So I'll guess we'll find out. Hey, maybe we can go on that trip. You never know.

*9.* Well, I'll tell you what, probably the day that he passed away. For about a year and a half he always had this oxygen on. Just fighting for breath. We were talking and all of a sudden he passed away. And then the nurse came in and unplugged the oxygen and it was just peaceful. You know, I could tell that he was in a better life, because he had suffered so much.

That's one of the things that I recall, the last time that I saw him. And it was just peaceful. I was sad because he was gone, but I also knew that he didn't want to be like he was.

*10.* You need to have a lot of patience. And be understanding. And listen. Listen to your kids—what they really have to say. A lot of people are ready to say things before they listen. So, I think one good trait is you have to listen real close and not make a quick, decisive, decision. And make sure it's right for everybody. That's one thing that I've tried to do.

That and there's one thing that I think I've been lacking some in and that is being more strict with them. I'm kind of a pushover. That's where my wife comes in. That's why when everybody says a man and a woman in a marriage, it does take two, and I think it takes two people that think alike. One is usually like myself, a little bit more submissive, and one that's more strict. If you can find a median there, that's best. Although the kids do have a tendency to come to ask me everything—because old Dad, he's the pushover. But then before the decision is made, usually my wife and I do talk and then make the decision. I think it takes two—not just a good father but also a good partner that thinks similarly. My wife and I don't think similarly in a lot of things, but when it comes to the kids, we are two people that want to get to the same place.

# CHAPTER 17

# Alfred

*Brother of John Henry and Ralph,*
*Uncle of Jason, Cousin of Richard*

*1.* Alfred, forty-eight.

*2.* Dad, because I felt that he was in a position of honor, and
that's why I did it.

*3.* Firm, because he was a big man and very authentic. He was
an authority figure because of being a big man.
Yes.

*4.* We were laying tile on the roof, and we had to do all the hard
work of scraping it off. And then he got up there and we had to
help lift the tiles up. Then he took the time to actually show us how
to lay them out, where to nail them, and what the final result was
supposed to look like. So it was hands on training.

*5.* Well, there's not one particular incident, but I'd say all the
farming that he did. When I was a little kid, I was always helping
him out and he let me drive the tractor. I was always proud of him
for what he did and how he fed the cattle and how he took care of
the family. That's probably the best example I can give.

*6.* Oh probably my feet. I wouldn't call it gout, but they crack a lot. I get my dry feet from my dad. So that's probably what I got the most of, and I don't like it. (Laughs.)

*7.* Since my dad worked out of town, every once in a while on a weekend, my mom and the rest of us kids would drive up to where he was working. And he would always take the time to take us kids and show us what he was doing as far as construction work and where he was working. And I'd always ask him how he operated the machinery, so he'd put me on the machinery and I'd get to play around.

*8.* I guess that I didn't think he was so giving and so trusting. Because in the later part of his life, when he got married the last time before he passed away, all of us kids could tell that this woman was taking advantage of him. And we couldn't portray that to him. He went to religion and forgave her and forgave her and forgave her up until the time he died. If he knew what she did the day after he died, he would roll over in his grave.

*9.* It would have to be when we were on the farm and he was filling the wheat truck. Once it started filling, he laid me up front on the top of the wheat and I actually fell asleep and didn't wake up until we got back to the house. I just enjoyed working with him on the farm when I was a little kid.

*10.* I want all fathers to show affection to their kids. Spend time with them, and let them know that Dad cares—but within certain boundaries. Discipline them and teach them the correct things while showing them that Dad still cares and loves them.

# CHAPTER 18

# John Henry

*Brother of Alfred and Ralph,*
*Uncle of Jason, Cousin of Richard*

*1.* John Henry. Fifty-two.

*2.* Called him Dad, all the time.

*3.* He tried to help everybody out. Anytime I needed help, he helped me out, with school and all that.

*4.* He taught me skills about farming, about raising chickens from the little ones up to seven weeks when they went out. It's something I didn't know, and some about gardening.

*5.* I was proud of my father when I found out that he had quit drinking and started teaching Sunday school. Then he started preaching some at church, and I was real proud of him for that.

*6.* I know I got my height from him because he was a tall person.

*7.* He was never afraid of doing anything. There were times when I rode with him in the vehicle, and water was flooded over the road. He just turned his windshield wipers on and drove right through it and water was half way up on the windshield. That's something that I would never do.

Drove right on through.

*8.* He surprised me because he wasn't afraid to do anything.

I was with him one day when the electricity went out—wire broke. He just pulled the meter out, got a pickup under there with two ladders, tied the ladders together, spliced the wire back, and put the meter back in.

*9.* On Sundays after church, we'd all pack up and go to the creek and have a little picnic and go swimming. I enjoyed that a lot.

*10.* If the kid gets into any trouble or anything, the father should sit and listen to him and try and help him out.

# CHAPTER 19

# Ralph

## Brother of Alfred and John Henry, Uncle of Jason, Cousin of Richard

*1.* Ralph. Forty-one.

*2.* Dad. What normally everybody calls his dad.

*3.* Tall, hard-working. Caring.
Yeah.

*4.* Building—we gutted out trailer houses and made dog kennels out of them—how to measure it, and the proper tools to use.

*5.* When I saw him get bucked off the horse. (Laughs.) At his age, he would still get on the horse; he was in his fifties. But I heard him hit the ground from fifty feet away. And he wasn't afraid. I rode the same horse.

*6.* Hard work, not to give up. Keep striving.

*7.* When he taught me how to water-ski at six years old. Every time we'd go to the lake, he'd clean the fish—until he and I caught too many.

*8.* There wasn't anything that surprised me.

*9.* It would be when we were out cutting hay or when he was helping John Henry and me when we were leasing that dairy farm in Oklahoma. He helped us out whenever we needed the help.

Also, I was the last family member to see my father alive. I had to go to town and pick up something and Dad was bush hogging around the field where we'd cut the tall grass so we could bail it to feed the cows.

And I came home, driving my little Datsun pickup, and noticed the tractor wasn't out there; he'd borrowed one because ours was broken. So I went inside to see if he was inside; he wasn't. I went back out to my truck and drove through our big gate that was made out of old wagon wheels.

The tractor was upside down. So we had to call, and the volunteer fire department came out. They tried everything to get the tractor off of him, but nothing worked. Finally they just got all the neighbor guys that were standing around watching to get a hold of the tractor and lift it up so they could get him out. But he was already ... It broke his neck. And he was all purple because it was over a hundred degrees. My step-mom took the car back, sold some of the stuff, and went on her merry way.

*10.* To keep striving for a goal that they want. For me, I probably wouldn't be at the job I'm at right now if it weren't for my kids. I got to keep going so I can take care of them.

# CHAPTER 20

# Joseph

*1.* Joseph, nineteen.

2. That's kind of funny because I call my dad Poppy Chulo. I don't know why. It's just something that popped up out of nowhere.

*3.* A workaholic, and a good father.
Oh, I do. Dad's always working.

*4.* When I was in the eighth grade, my dad taught me how to play the trumpet—very poorly. It was kind a hard because he was always working. But he'd get off about two o'clock in the morning, wake me up and say, "Let's go play." So we'd sit out in the back yard and get all our neighbors screaming at us, because we played the trumpet very badly and late.

*5.* Loving my mom, staying with her, instead of splitting up like they had planned to.

*6.* I'd definitely have to say my dad's workaholic sense of nature. He works a lot. And I got a job now that I work twenty-four hours a day, seven days a week. So, I'd say that's one of the main things I picked up from him.

7. It would definitely have to be about their yearly trips with Mailers With Trailers, a little organization he's got at work now. We all go out to a pre-set campsite with a bunch of mailers—my dad's co-workers—and we've all got RV trailers, fifth wheels, pop-ups, what have you. There's about forty of us at a time, making a big horseshoe. And we're all just getting trashed for two weeks straight, having a grand old time.

8. Wow. I don't know. I really don't have an answer for that one. He's the same guy.

9. Fishing, when I was eight up on Lake Pleasant. It was a perfectly clear sky, no clouds. It was probably about eight o'clock in the morning. We'd driven out there the night before and stayed out there on the lake about four or five hours—just fishing, him and me. And then we went back to pick up my brother and we did the same thing the next day. It was great.

10. Dependability, most definitely. Dependability and integrity.

# CHAPTER 21

# Clark

*1.* My interview name is Clark, fifty-four.

*2.* I call him Dad. That's what I've always called him. I don't know if there's a way I arrived at it—it always seemed to be Dad. Not Daddy too much, but Dad.

*3.* He would be described as having great integrity, stick-to-itiveness. He was a take-charge kind of guy. His job made him in charge of a lot of people and they all seemed to like him and like his management style—there were people that didn't like him too much, but basically a lot of integrity, a lot of stick-to-itiveness, trustworthy. A good guy.

Yes I do.

*4.* (Laughs.) Can it be recent? This is like a right of passage for me. My joke about my father is when he did things, I always got to hold the flashlight rather than actually get in and do stuff. He had surgery just this last year and he became incapacitated; he couldn't use his arms, couldn't lift more than five pounds. He has a fireplace and they use the fireplace a lot in the winter. He spent two weeks before the surgery cutting as much wood as he could, until he had the surgery. Then he burned all that, so I went up.

I have never gotten to use the chainsaw in my life. Fifty-four years old and he's never let me use the chainsaw. Not when I was a teenager going out in the woods, not when I was in college. I always got to split the wood with a sledgehammer. As his wife says, "Nobody gets to use the chainsaw."

And he told me, "Nobody ever uses the chainsaw. When they want to borrow my chainsaw, they borrow me." So here I am fifty-four years old and we're trying to put in wood and I said, "Dad, let me use the chainsaw."

He said, "You're gonna cut your leg off. I'm just afraid you'll cut your leg off."

I said, "Nobody has any more vested interest in keeping my leg than I do. I will be as cautious as I can." He really groused about it. But he finally gave in. He told me exactly what to do and watched me like a hawk and made sure I pulled the cord right and did everything right.

I had my rite of passage like boys that get the Christmas turkey. Finally at age fifty-four, I got to use my dad's chainsaw. It was just his whole manner. He stood next to me and watched me. He passed me the piece of wood, stood there, and watched me.

"Okay, you did it good that time."

So basically when he taught me something, it was always stand over my shoulder and make sure I didn't cut my leg off, or put the fishhook in my ear, or whatever. That's how I remember him teaching me things.

5. Aw man. There are lots. I'm proud of my dad in a lot of ways. I've always been proud of my dad's accomplishments and there have been many. I think about his success in the business he was in, and the fact that he advanced as far as he had wanted to. And then that he's been able to continue on after he'd retired, doing the things he likes, the things he enjoys.

Again more recently, it's just the way that he's gone through this surgery and all the things that happened to him during that. And to see the stages he went through. I'm just really proud of the way that he's been able to go through it. We're talking about a physically active guy who's in his seventies and never wanted people to do anything for him.

I think the proudest moment, it may seem a little silly, was the first time I went up after the surgery. He couldn't drive, so I drove him. He wanted to get out and go to Wal-Mart; he hadn't been to the new Wal-Mart. We made him take his walker because he was very unstable. He had neck surgery and if he fell, he'd run the risk of damaging himself. So we went to Wal-Mart and he was in the walker. And we came back and he put the walker up and said, "I'm never using this again," he told his wife. "So you might as well just give it to Goodwill."

So we went to Wal-Mart the next day without the walker. He got a cart and he used the cart as a walker. But that made him feel so old and decrepit. I'm just very proud of how he's handling this adjustment to his life and the way he's maybe coming to grips with his own mortality. I'm not going to deal with it very well; I can tell you that right now.

6. I think that I picked up a love for reading, a love for knowledge. Any discipline I have in my life, I picked up from him because he was a strict disciplinarian and demanded that I have a code of ethics; live your life by being as good a person as you can, and treat people with as much respect as you can. All those qualities that I see in him, he's tried to instill in me; and I've picked those up from him. I don't think I can match him, but I've tried pretty hard to do those things.

Whatever religious feelings and belief I have, I've picked up from him. The feelings for family, and maybe even some of being a bit cranky at times, I've picked up from him too because of the way he handles situations.

Patience and stubbornness—I picked up those from him. I would like to think that most of the good things about me as a person, I've picked up from him. He educated me in my formative years—I'm an only child.

7. Again, a recent story. This is one of my favorite stories just because of the total silliness of the whole thing. With all the surgery and everything that he went through, he had a spell where he

would just say things you didn't expect him to say. There is a term for it—they call it ICU silliness.

Dad was in this situation, and again we came very close to losing him. That's why I went up, because when he went into the ICU, they said he was never coming out. He proved them wrong. But anyway, he would be lucid at times, but some of the things that he said in his unlucidness would just crack me up. Even though they were kind of bad in a way and all the while I'm going, I hope he works his way out of this.

He would talk about how he lived on the streets and my dad has never been homeless or anything like that. But he lived on the streets and slept under trucks and he worked in a diamond mine. He'd say all kinds of things like that.

The other funny thing was he really wanted to get out of the hospital. He didn't want to be there. And he looked at me and he grabbed my hand and said, "C'mon, unhook me! Go pay the bill and get me out of here."

I said, "Dad, I can't do that."

And then he looked at me and said, "Well then you are a dork." (Laughs.) Now my dad has never called me a dork knowingly to my face; he may have thought it, but there were four other people in the room. The way he said it just struck me funny, while at the same time I was hoping he would snap out of it.

But the funniest thing was he kept talking about being homeless, living on the streets and all this. The nurse came in and did some stuff and he looked at me and said, " I learned one thing when I lived on the streets of Calcutta. Don't listen to anything strange women tell you."

That just cracks me up every time I hear it. Just out of nowhere. "Don't listen to anything strange women tell you." It cracks me up now that he's lucid and remembers everything and everything's back to normal. We kind of laugh at it now—he doesn't remember it. He says, "I was in La-La-Land for a while." That's his explanation.

*8.* I was really surprised that he was not that tied to his job. I pegged him as somebody who, because he worked so hard, would do a Bear Bryant and die right after he retired. And I always kind of worried about that. He's been retired for years; he retired at sixty-two. He's seventy-eight right now, and going great guns. And we've talked about it.

"Why did you retire?" I asked.

He said, "Well, I tired of what they were doing. I loved it and I stopped loving it. So I retired."

That was one of those things; I had always lived with this belief that he was so tied to his work, and he wasn't. It sort of became this burden to him and he didn't like it so he decided to go do something else. And he has. And that was something I didn't know.

My dad says he's busier now than when he was working. He's very active in the church and lending himself out to help people cut wood. (Laughs.) He always finds something to do. It's great. I think it's that generation; you're talking depression era.

*9.* I have lots of those, which one to pick? The first thing that came to my mind was fishing when I was a kid. We used to go out to a lake by where we lived out on the dam and go fishing. We did that quite often. All the fishing trips we took, didn't catch much, but that's okay; we had fun. We'd sit there and he'd tell me to be quiet. Later on, we had a rowboat, and all that stuff.

Our little fishing excursions come to mind right away. There were many others but that one zeroed right in.

Another favorite story just came to me—a funny story. My dad would do this little thing, to always prove that he was the guy in charge. When I was in junior high, maybe freshman in high school, he'd come home and for just for no reason, he'd slug me in the arm. And he'd be smiling, "C'mon, hit me back."

And I'd hit him back and he'd just laugh, "That's not hard." It was just little game we played to freak my mom out all the time. And he didn't do it every day. He'd come home sometimes and I'd start him up too, "C'mon, c'mon, hit me, hit me."

But I guess one day I got him pretty hard because he turned

around and hit me right in the crotch and I passed out, fell on the floor. "Breathe, you'll be okay," he said. "You're not hurt." (Laughs.)

Every once in a while he'd do things like that to me. Sometimes we'd wrestle. I remember one time in high school he had my friend in a full-nelson and he had me in a leg wrap thing and I couldn't move and my friend couldn't move. He just sat there and laughed at us. He said, "Big high school kids, and you can't handle an old man." That was his way of being the big bear that swats the cubs around to remind them who is in charge.

*10.* I would say that devotion isn't too strong a word. I think fathers need to have that responsibility toward the family and toward their kids. I say this not as a father myself, but it isn't necessarily the amount of time that you spend. Knowing my dad and other people I consider to be successful fathers, it's that you have quality time with your kids all through their life.

And it continues on, no matter how old you get. You don't end up like that Harry Chapin song where you're too busy for each other; you've got that time. I think that is the most important because you don't want any regrets about not being with your kids, not being with your dad.

I'd say devotion, dedication. Being there for your kids and your family. Making that time quality time, not just a paycheck.

# CHAPTER 22

# Bill

*1.* My name is Bill, and thirty-two.

*2.* Dad. (Laughs.) I guess that's just what I was asked to call him.

*3.* (Laughs.) Depends who you talk to. Some people would say controlling in some aspects. Friendly, sometimes more sociable than others, more sociable around people he knows than people that he doesn't know. Strong willed. Strong personality. He's very much a wants-to-take-charge kind of person.

Well, probably some of the tendencies that I have to be controlling and strong-willed, I got from him. So I think it can be a good thing, but if I let it control me, then a bad thing. Or let it control the situation or try to control other people—that's where the negative is.

*4.* I guess I can relate it back to my first experience out on the shooting range when my father tried to teach me how to shoot a gun. He's definitely not a very patient person, and in dealing with guns you have a tendency to over-react, and that's probably a good thing. But he's definitely not the teacher type.

He said, "I'll show you how to do it once or twice. You try it, and if you don't do it, well then you need to work on it on your own time." He's not the kind of person that would sit down and say this is how you need to do it, and be very patient and very reassuring.

He wasn't. (Laughs.) That's what I remember; that goes with anything he ever tried to teach me.

5. There have been quite a few. The one that stands out the most and defines why I'm proud of him was in my sophomore year of high school, my mom decided to leave. This wasn't the first time, but this was the final time. He told me the morning before as I was leaving to go to school. I had a football game that night—that's how I remember it, relate everything back to sports. He said she was leaving and asked if I wanted to go. I said no.

My dad really stepped in and basically became both mother and father and raised me. And then, about four months later, my younger brother came down to visit for Christmas, and decided to stay because he wanted to be with his big brother.

So as far as being proud, I would have to say he stepped in and filled the gap for me and my brother; he was both mother and father and supported us, raised us, brought us up, and took care of us. He didn't always make the right choices or decisions, but I don't know too many people who do.

6. (Laughs.) Probably lack of patience. But for some reason or another, going through a few relationships before I got married, I actually learned to work on that. The problem before was either my lack of patience, or my temper. I had a very quick temper. I saw my father lose his temper many times, and it was always something that I had a tendency to do. And I always saw that as something that I needed to work on. Even my father had said that to me a few times, "You don't want to end up like me and lose your temper." Maybe he just thought he was too old to change, but it was something that I've seen him work on a lot. And for me, something that was a bad thing, but has turned into a positive.

Dad remarried, and my two stepbrothers are younger; one is now twenty years old, so at the time they got married, he was still in high school. And I remember some of the stuff that my stepbrother did and my dad did not react in the way that he reacted to me. I noticed that he was definitely more patient, and not quite as temperamental. So I have seen a big change in my dad since my brother and I have grown up and moved out of the house.

And yet as a grandfather, it's taken him a while to warm up; I don't why that is. But in the last year, it's really been a big difference. I don't know if he was scared, or didn't know how to be a grandfather, or maybe thought he was too young; he just didn't know how to handle the situation.

Now he's really turned around and has done an awesome job. He's more patient with my son than he is with me.

7. There's so many—back to the grandfather thing. My mother's father, who I never met, left when my mom was twelve. For years and years, my mom never saw him after that day. He was gone; that was it. I've heard a lot of stories about what a great guy he was. But I didn't know what exactly happened, and why he left. When I got married about five years ago, I started doing some investigating. I started asking, "Who am I? Where am I? Where did I come from? Who was he?" I never met the man. "Was he still alive?"

And that's when I found out he died in 1985. Somehow I got his social security number and did a search on it and found out that he had died. Later, talking to my grandmother, she actually knew that, but never passed that information on to my mother or myself. My grandmother has been remarried since my mother was about thirteen, and she has two kids with her current husband and they have been married for thirty-eight years. I guess she didn't want to talk about it, and buried it in the past.

I remember specifically asking her on my wedding night, "What's the deal?" And she sat down and we talked for quite a long time. I heard stuff about him and how he was and the kind of guy he was. There were a lot of positives and there were a lot of negatives about him. He was an alcoholic and was physically abusive. But there were a lot of positive characteristics in him as well.

The grandfather that I did have was my dad's father, and he was always active. I can remember back to one story in particular, I was four years old, and the house we were living in had some citrus trees in the front yard. I picked up an old orange and not intentionally, by accident, threw that old orange through the front window of the house. And my dad, as I mentioned before, had a very short temper. (Laughs.) And he lost it. I just remember him yelling and screaming and just how scared I was.

Well my grandfather happened to come over at that time and it was funny how my dad would really change around my grandfather. Almost like he was scared of him, scared to act like an idiot in front of him. And I remember being upset and my grandfather going, "C'mon, let's go get some ice cream." And he took me down to Dairy Queen to get a dilly bar.

My grandfather's still alive, and he's actively involved in my son's life. My son is two and absolutely loves him; I hope my grandfather lives for a few more years so my son really gets to know who he is. It's so neat to see. Now we have four generations. My grandmother keeps saying, "We need to take a picture; we need to go in." We had a couple pictures done, but I'd like to go in and get one done professionally, because that's pretty special. I don't know too many people that have four generations of their family around.

8. I never saw a great relationship between my father and my mother. Years ago, my dad just got into doing what his father did and was a construction worker; he was a bricklayer. At that time, I saw what other people did that worked with them and what was expected. You know, work hard, party hard. He worked Monday through Friday, did side jobs on Saturday and Sunday and was at the bar Friday and Saturday night and back to work again on Monday. So I didn't really see my mother and him interact very much. I just assumed that he couldn't do that, or didn't know how.

And now that he is remarried and with his current wife, one thing that I see that really surprises me is that he has given in. He's become softer, I guess because of his age and dealing with things in his life while realizing problems that he suffered with earlier.

So I guess the biggest thing that's surprised me was seeing how he's really changed and has the ability to be more sensitive, and be more intuitive to his current wife's needs rather than just his own.

*9.* Wow, there's so many. I'd have to say the first time we went hunting together sticks out the most. My mother stayed at home; everybody else stayed at home. It was me, my dad, and a friend of his; it was just the three of us. It wasn't so much about whether we got something or didn't. It was just that we got to spend time together. We got to get out in the woods and just be together.

As I think back to my childhood, that's probably one of the biggest things that stands out. Sometimes he wasn't very good about spending time with us at home, but we grew up camping, or hunting, or riding motorcycles and quads. We did a lot of that together.

*10.* I have a tendency to want to get involved in projects around the house. I have to keep myself busy and constantly working. It's something that I suffer from; it's just my personality, and it's something that my wife and I have talked about a lot. One thing that I have a hard time with is to spend enough quality time with my son. I've been working on it; it's a struggle. I have to really think about it to do it.

Granted he's two-and-a-half right now, so it's a little hard to go out and play ball. And he has the attention span of a gnat, so it's a little hard sometimes to sit down because he doesn't want to sit and he's constantly moving.

But I would have to say the biggest thing is time. You've got to spend time with your kids. And it's not just being in the room or being there while they're there that's important. I think you have to interact and actually be involved in what they are doing, or have to say, or how they're feeling. My dad was always there as far as being there physically. But sometimes I felt, at least when I got older, his ability to communicate wasn't always there. If I had something that was bothering me or troubling me, I didn't feel that I could necessarily go to him.

But I could go to my grandfather. I saw a lot of characteristics in my grandfather that I think are absolutely necessary in a father. In talking to my dad, grandfather wasn't always like that, so maybe that's a growth thing. I've tried to use all I've learned from my father and my grandfather to be a better father to my son.

My dad and mom had me when they were twenty. They were rather young. I think back to when I was twenty. I definitely would have been a different father than I am now, because of maturity level, age and life experiences.

I'm really trying to work on the relationship between my father and me. And it's just recently that we've gotten a lot closer than we had been. Earlier this year, we didn't talk for about six months; I was ticked that he wasn't spending enough time or even acknowledging my son. All that has changed a lot. And there are a lot of reasons for it.

CHAPTER 23

# Clayton

*1.* Clayton. Age, sixty-two.

*2.* I call him Dad. And I'm not sure how I arrived at it. It wasn't a structured thing. I wasn't going to call him by his first name; that wasn't going to happen.

*3.* They would describe him as a hard, working man. He was a man who took care of his family. He was amiable, a good-natured person, and a Christian. He went to church throughout his life and grew up in the country.

Well, yeah. Yeah.

*4.* My father taught me how to fix a flat on a tire, a long time ago when I was a kid. The most recent was when I was twenty-five and I got my first building. He taught me how to do a lot of repairs, general maintenance and how to keep things operational, mainly electrical and plumbing. He showed me, and then he let me do it. If I didn't do it right, I had to do it again.

He taught me everything about baseball. And of course the behavior patterns of what you can and can't do in this world and what he wasn't going to allow. There were differences there between what the police allowed and what he allowed. The police allowed more for sure.

5. One day years ago, a gentleman who's a Senator now in Illinois, fell in a manhole in the street where they were doing some work. He was trapped down there; he and I were about the same age, twelve. My father reached down in the sewer and risked his own life to help the boy. Right after he pulled this kid out of there, the sewer collapsed, which would have killed the boy. And if it had happened while my father was down there, it would have killed them both.

That boy's a minister now-a-days and he's also a state Senator. In fact, he was down in that manhole a while because they were saying, "Wait, wait," and my father was coming home from work and they were all standing around the manhole. He went right in to get that boy out of there; he wasn't going to wait for the fire department and the rest of them. This Senator has a television church program, and when he goes to his sermon, every once in a while he reaches back to that day he was saved by my father and he'll mention my father's name on television. He even came to my father's funeral.

6. Everything I know how to do I got from my father, except for my formal education. Of course, for that I had to go to school. But my father taught me everything there was to know about working, cleaning house, fixing electrical and plumbing, and this was a self-educated man.

He went to school to the third grade, and then his dad pulled him out of school and put the kids to work. He did go to night school—pattern drafting, and there was another course. I'm not sure how long he went to school.

But he taught me almost everything that was necessary to maintain a house. Of course, there are some areas you don't touch. You don't mess with the furnace if it shuts down; you call a professional. But my father taught me a great deal.

7. My father and my mother took me to New York to live. I don't know if you've been there, but a lot of the streets look familiar. I was only ten years old at the time. And naturally I was joking with

my father and teasing him and my father challenged me. He said, "Well, let's do this thing." We were in downtown New York. And I lived on Forty-sixth Street, a long way, over a hundred blocks from where we were. And I didn't realize this and I was walking ahead of my father.

My father said, "Why are you walking so fast?"

"Well, we're almost home," I told him.

He said. "No, you're not almost home."

I thought he was trying to trick me into submission and saying, "Okay. We'll catch the bus." And I kept on walking and he let me just walk straight on ahead.

After a while, he caught up with me and he said, "Are you sure you want to walk? We've been walking a while now."

I said, "Yeah, we're going to walk. We're almost home now. There's so and so's house and there's just the next few blocks."

He said, "It's not that close." I thought he was jiving me. I didn't think he was lying; he was just jiving.

He wasn't jiving me. (Laughs.) We'd only gone about twenty blocks, and we still had a hundred blocks to go and he let me. He didn't try to stop me anymore; he walked with me.

I was thinking that because I was a little kid, this is one way I might be able to sneak up on my father. He was fierce and what have you, and I was going to show him I was grown. (Laughs.) He made me walk the hundred and twenty blocks. Of course my mother gave him the blues when we got home because my side was hurting and I was feeling a lot of pain. I went to bed and didn't wake up until the next day. (Laughs.)

8. My father had worked in a steel mill years before as a chipper, someone who removes the excess parts off the steel with a torch. He was still living at the time, and I was going through his things trying to help him get organized. My father couldn't work and they were having problems paying their bills, not because they didn't have the money; my mama just took them and put them on the table for somebody else and then didn't go about paying them. And when I picked up a bill one day, I remarked there was a big

notice from ConEd, the electric company, and Hoover Gas—they sent cut-off notices. And the homeowner's and the auto insurance hadn't been renewed. And there were several months that had passed and these bills hadn't been paid.

I was going by on a regular basis; I just didn't see the mail, because it was kept in the bedroom. Not that I didn't go in there, but I didn't go in there looking under the tablecloth and everything else.

But at this time, I realized he also had a letter from the steel mill where he had worked. They were supposed to have this dinner and a special kind of award for him for inventing this tool that they didn't have before. He had made it himself for handling these big pieces of steel that rolled out when he was chipping. I followed up on it and I wrote a letter to the company, because from what I understand, they said there was going to be this dinner and award to honor him. But they didn't have the dinner; nor did he get an award.

I followed up on it again, and I wrote the company another letter and of course it took the company a while to get it, because US Steel on the south side of Chicago had closed down their plant and were going back to Pennsylvania. When I finally got a letter back it was, "We're sorry, blah, blah. We have no records of this." They said it was because he did not have a pattern of the tool. If he or I had a pattern for the tool, I could have pursued the award for him. I was trying to find out why he didn't get the bonus or whatever he was supposed to get, and of course that is where it ended. But I was surprised to hear he had invented something, and that he received some acknowledgement for it; this was a man with thirty years in the business.

*9.* When I was around the age of ten in Illinois, my father used to go and get night crawlers out of the ground to go fishing. I wanted to go. I was ten and I wanted to stay up late, and especially to go out at night with a flashlight to pick up worms. Oh, yeah. I did that.

And the next morning, he got me up and took me out there. It's

called Wolf Lake. Actually I wasn't interested in fishing, too boring. I mean you had to put the worm on the thing, throw it out in
the water, and sit and wait for something to happen. After we were
there for a while, I laid the pole down. I had on cut off pants, and
next thing you know I ran and jumped into the water right in the
area where we were fishing. And he said, "How you going to catch
a fish when you're going to scare them all away by your ruckus?"

I wasn't half listening and said, "Well, I don't want to fish; I
don't like fishing anyway," not thinking I was disturbing him catching fish too. So I splashed around in the water for a good fifteen
minutes, and when I looked around again, he had walked away and
left me there. The car was there with our stuff; the fishing pole of
mine was there, but he was gone. We had sandwiches in the car, but
I had no idea where he went. I was scared at first when I looked
down the long aisle that goes through the middle of Wolf Lake
and I didn't see him. I played in the water a little longer. I told myself, "He is gone, but he'll come back."

Five hours passed. When he came back, I was asleep in the
back seat of the car; he didn't wake me up as he put the stuff in the
car. I guess it was around six o'clock; it was getting to be dusk by
then. He woke me later and said, "You won't be going fishing with
me anymore." (Laughs.)

"I don't want to go fishing anymore," I told him.

Then I caught myself telling on him, "Momma, Daddy left me
when I jumped in the water. He left me down there, and I didn't
know where he went."

I'm thinking my mother is going to fuss at him and she says to
me, "You can't go fishing. You are supposed to be fishing with your
father. You are not supposed to scare the fish away."

My dad taught me lessons that may have seemed dangerous. I
didn't know it at the time, but my dad was fishing where he could
see me; I just couldn't see him. He didn't miss one way of getting
the lessons across. He didn't have to give spankings or any threats;
he'd just leave me to my own demise.

There is another time when he took me shopping downtown to
Sears, but I wanted to go to see the toys. When I would go down-

town with my mother she would say, "We have to go pay these bills first, then I'll take you to see the toys."

My dad wasn't going to tell me that. He said, "You wanted to come down here with me," because he knew I just wanted to go so I could tell him that I wanted to go to see the toys. He said, "No, you stay right here." He didn't grab my hand or anything. He said, "You stay right here until I finish conducting my business. If we have time, I may let you see some toys."

Well, little old energetic me was running at this and looking at that, and I was thinking he is here; out of my peripheral I could see his figure. And the next thing you know, I came around the corner of the store, and I couldn't see him and I really got scared. I was thinking he left me down here. But he also told me, "If you don't stay here, when I get ready to go, I am not going to look for you. I can tell you that right now; I am not going to look for you when it is time for me to go."

I fell out on the floor just kicking and crying out loud, folks looking down at me saying, "What's wrong with this child?"

"I can't find my daddy," I said. And they decided to take me up to lost and found. This lady got me up off the floor and I was still crying. She gave me a Kleenex and she was walking with me and holding my hand.

We didn't even get up to the steps of the escalator when my father appeared and said, "That's my son. It's time for him to go home now." I looked right at him, but I didn't say a word all the way home because I knew I didn't do what he told me to do. If they had asked him, he probably would have told them, "Keep the boy at Sears." I thought he had left me.

10. To put the needs and wants of the child first. That's the one thing. My dad wanted to do a lot of things for me. He said, "I could do some things for you; it's not a matter of money. It's not a matter of ability; it's a matter of what's best for you." Case in point—we had to keep our own rooms and help out around the house. He told my mother, "You don't help the child at any time."

He could have sent me to college without me playing basketball. My playing basketball simply gave him a little money back. That was my way of helping me out, or for him to help me. Of course, my dad was never one to tell me he was going to do something if he didn't think he could. He would say, "If I tell you I'm going to do something, unless I die, yes I'll do it." Even up to the point when Dad died at ninety, that's the kind of trust and confidence that I had in him.

That's the one thing he taught me that I tell my children; if I said it, they knew that they could count on me. I wasn't afraid to say I don't know right now. And I wasn't afraid to say if there was something I didn't know how to do.

I have a brother who leaves a lot to be desired. He has four beautiful children, and they call me up and ask me to talk to him when he does something they don't particularly like. I'm not my brother's keeper, but I've talked with him.

To me he's a disappointment. Every one of his kids ran away in high school and they were making good grades and they were smart. But he didn't have anything to give them because he was too selfish. Maybe he wants to act like a kid, but I just told him to stop, "You better quit lying to yourself and look at things the way they are. Your family doesn't trust you or have confidence in your ability to do the things you need to do."

He's fifty-seven now, and he's missing out. My daughter calls me just to say, "Hi," and she wants to laugh and talk with me. His daughter will talk to him, but it's not a thing that she wants and she gives him one-word responses. She doesn't want him in her life. I find it encouraging that my daughter wants to talk to me about some boy that likes her and she doesn't feel I'm a big ogre.

When she was younger, I told her, "If they come over here and they have a rag on their head, they have to go back home and change if they want to go out with you." And she thought that was kind of stiff. And I replied, "And maybe it is. But you have to know that he better not come here with a doo-rag on his head and looking like a hoodlum, because you don't date hoodlums." She got the message. She knew I cared about whom she went out with, and would make sure they took care of her and treated her right.

I told her, "I'll pick my friends, and you pick yours. I don't have to like yours and you don't have to like mine. But you have to be respectful." And I treat her friends with respect. How come many of them want to come by and talk to me if I'm supposed to be so bad? That was encouragement for me. I enjoy the kids; I'm getting older, but I can still contribute to the conversation.

# CHAPTER 24

# Wes

*1.* My interview name is Wes, and my age is fifty-seven.

*2.* I call my dad, Daddy, because he didn't like to be called Pop or Poppa so it was always Daddy—to this day.

*3.* Happy-go-lucky. Cheerful. Never met a stranger.
Yes, a lot.

*4.* Ye-ah. (Laughs.) He said, "Well, we're going to build this barn. I want you to use a hammer and nails." And we set it out. The first thing I did was hit my thumb and broke it and he had to take me to the doctor's. And he said. "That's enough of that. (Laughs.) Let's do this when you get a little older." I was ten. Still hurts. (Laughs.)

*5.* We were getting off the school bus, and this old drunk came around and started fooling around with the kids. My father was driving behind the bus. He got out of his car and he gave the man a ride home. And he told us kids that we'd be just fine. I was so proud of him because we were scared.

*6.* His carefree way, his big smile, shaking everybody's hand. And he always used their name—I don't know how he remembered everybody's name—but he always remembered everybody's name. So I try to do that, too.

7. Well, my dad was a pilot and he had a Cessna 180 and he had a twelve seater Otter. And he took me up for a flight. Actually, he wanted to show all of us kids how to fly. So we were all on the plane and my mother came running out of the house screaming, "You're not taking my family up in that plane. Ever!" So only I went. All the other siblings had to get off. (Laughs.)

But we flew. We flew from where we lived in Edmunds all the way to Vancouver, British Columbia and back again. And I got to hear the tower in Los Angeles telling him where he was and where he could land and all that.

It was a seaplane, so it was pretty remarkable; I was twelve years old and I got to fly it. You know, just hold the thing in the air and raise it. It was really phenomenal. (Laughs.)

8. When I was forty, I went home. My dad said, "I haven't seen you for a while. I want to go for a walk with you." So he grabbed my hand like I was five years old and we started walking and he started telling me everything about my life and how he was so proud of me, which blew my mind. I was surprised. It was something that made me feel remarkable. Not many people do that for you. (Laughs.) Especially when there are eight children.

And he did it with each and every one of us. (Laughs.) I mean, it's phenomenal. I wasn't the only one. We all started talking after he died and everybody said, " He did the same thing last year." I wonder if he knew he was going to be gone soon. And the night before he died, he called me on the phone, as if a premonition. I don't know. But it was closure for me.

"Hey Wes," He said.

I said, "Yeah Dad." (Laughs.) And he just talked for hours, and just about me, not about him. And he'd come from such a big family—five boys and eleven girls besides him.

Incredible. But he was very loving. He'd see you and he'd grab you and kiss you on the cheek, both cheeks, and he would hold you tight and you'd get embarrassed sometimes. After a while, it didn't matter. That's your dad. He was incredible.

*9*. Like I said, the last time I was with him was, "Let's go for a walk," and we walked down on the farm and sat down on the bench by the barn. He said, "You know, we should go fishing again."

And I said, "Yeah." I had just lost my wife, so it was kind of a rough time for me and he was supporting me and keeping everything off my mind.

*10*. Gosh, that's hard. I think all fathers should tell their boys how much they love them. Or show it in some way, like my dad did, hug you every morning. Darn it, it's a wonderful thing, you know? Because you have so much stuff with just being, it didn't matter how big you were or how little you were. You were up here (puts hand above head) every day. It was incredible.

# CHAPTER 25

# Carlos

*1.* Carlos and fifty-one in two days.

*2.* His name has always been Dad. I don't know. I've never thought about that one. I've never considered anything else but Dad.

*3.* Of course it depends on who knows him. He was always thought of by a large section of people, as a very loving, generous, and funny man. Others recognized his phoniness—he was phony. He was insecure, didn't like himself. His closest friends probably knew that one.

I saw both sides of him. I knew exactly when people were talking about him being a funny man, or a loving man. I think only as an adult did I start to realize that he had some very insecure issues. He had a serious problem about his being a Mexican—the whole issue of him trying to be better than everybody else. He tried to be successful in the White world. And he liked to kind of show that off to the other Mexicans while still keeping his heritage. And he still wanted to live in both worlds—he wanted to be big in both worlds.

And I think I now understand his phoniness, because he was a big phony. I consider him the biggest phony I have known. His phoniness was the result of his insecurities, of his not liking himself, just wanting to be somebody else. Because that's what phony is.

I saw my father in action. And later on I realized, like so many other people like that, "Why do you have to be that way? Because you're fine the way you are." But he obviously wasn't happy with who he was.

4. There are definitely things I do that I learned from him. My dad taught me how to drive. He worked at a car dealership, so he had access to cars. And I worked at the car dealership when I got my license. But he would take me out and like most other fathers, teach gently at first, but quickly get frustrated to the point where I remember him actually having to pull over as I dropped him off. Then he let me drive through an industrial neighborhood on my own; it just got to the point where I was too nervous and he was too freaking out. But in the meantime, him just giving me the car on my own gave me what I needed to learn to drive.

5. I was always proud of my father when he exhibited the love that I knew he had towards my son or my daughter or my wife. I was proud when I would see that he would give anything for another person.

When my mom's father had a stroke—she was one of ten children, of course all adults at this time—my dad was the only one that would take my grandfather into his house. My grandfather had a stroke to the point where he was incapable of anything, really. He reverted back to a four year old and he told you he was a four year old if you asked him. He required twenty-four hour watching—they had to lock him in the room because he would get out and escape. He was unable to be in a home.

But I watched my father give him showers, clean up his shit, just do everything that none of his own sons would do. And that's huge. Dad gave up a whole summer sleeping in the same room as my out-of-control grandfather, which meant he didn't sleep with my mom for a whole summer. And he didn't get much sleep. He did what I couldn't have done.

6. My dad enjoyed being with other people. I don't know if once again, it had to do with him being insecure with himself and wanting to impress other people, but he really enjoyed interacting with others. Even though he was very, very, unhappy with himself, he seemed to enjoy little things in life. I've noticed that I'm not very hard to please and I didn't get the impression that he was that hard to please either.

I think what I got from my father was his loyalty. I watched him be extremely loyal even through flaming alcoholism and everything else. Being loyal to his brothers, to us, to my mom, to his friends—I think that was one of his strongest points. I would have never thought about it myself, but it's been pointed out that I'm a very loyal person. So I think that's something I picked up from him. I can't think of anybody that he disowned or was conditional with in terms of giving somebody something. It was all basically unconditional.

7. I have very, very strong memories of him taking me to my first professional football game when I was ten years old. We went down to San Diego to watch the Chargers when they were in the old AFL. I don't remember a whole lot other than the fact that we went with somebody else. But he took me to the game and did the things that a father typically does, and he bought me a souvenir—I think it was a sweatshirt. I just had a really good time and thought that was the coolest thing. To this day, watching the Chargers still takes me back to that first game.

8. I think when I really discovered that he based who he was on the fact that he didn't like himself. I didn't grow up thinking that he didn't like himself. That was something that I learned a little later on. And it was something that put the whole picture into perspective. I mean, there were a whole lot of times when I was angry for what he did, when I didn't understand what he did, and when I thought it was so grossly wrong. It didn't take away a lot of the pain. It didn't take away any anger at what he had done to other

people, but at least I understood it. So, that was something that I didn't learn until I was an adult.

*9.* One Christmas he fought it, once again, bringing up his alcoholism. He swore he was an alcoholic as a high school student, but he wasn't out of control. In his later years, he'd go back and forth; he'd attempt to stop so that he could stay with the family, and then he'd fall off the wagon.

There was one time during Christmas and New Years that he and I went to a Fiesta Bowl together. It was the last time he visited us in Phoenix. And it was cool to just spend the afternoon with him. I took him down to Tempe for the first time; we grabbed something to eat at the Coffee Plantation and walked over to Sun Devil Stadium. It was a pleasant memory. I think it was one of the last times I spent with him when he was sober.

*10.* I think it's unconditional love. I can't even think about not having that with my kids.

# CHAPTER 26

# Salmen

*1.* I am forty-two years old. I am Salmen.

*2.* I call him, not Dad or Poppa. I call him something which pretty much means Dad in my native language, Abba. Just heard it from my other sister I guess. (Laughs.) Follow the rules, I guess. (Laughs.)

*3.* Very helpful to the people and hard working—and head of the family actually back there. When anyone has any problems, they usually call him for the solution. When I grew up, I called my dad by a different name, which is like brother, because I was living in a joint family system back in Pakistan. And my father's brothers and sister were living with us, so they called him Brother, so I started calling him Brother.

But then I grew up and they said, "You cannot say that if he's your dad." I have to say it sometimes, but I'm very hesitant.

He is to the family members. If somebody comes to him and asks for help, he always tries to help people, friends and family and everybody else.

*4.* Everybody goes to school, but he was the one when I was very young who taught me my native language in depth, like grammar and everything. But when I was very, very young, I could actually write and read much before the others of that age. I think at six, seven years old, pretty much, I could write everything in my native language which is very rare at that age in that country. People don't do that a lot at that age. That was very nice.

Plus he taught me how to live. He was a self-made man. So he showed me how to make it—it's very hard—but he showed me how. Sometimes he was very harsh on me. He feels that when I was a young kid, I missed a lot, such as playing on the streets, because of do this, do that. And because I was always pretty much with him working on my days off from school. Summer vacation, he took me out to the office to work. I started working actually at a very early age; I think I was in fourth grade. He had an office in the publishing company, plus he had a printing press and a binding section. He showed me how everything worked.

Talking about the publisher, when I was fourteen years old, I could publish a book. I knew all the forms. I know how to take all the films. I can actually do that.

I was just going to high school when he got really sick and I had to go in and work in the office. He had forty or fifty people working for him at that time. It's very hard to manage an opinion when you are so young and to go and sit in an office. I was very fortunate because I knew all about it and they knew that I knew all about it. So they couldn't escape me or tell me, no this is not right, or something like that.

I was able to run the business for quite a while. He had a peptic ulcer and he had to be hospitalized for a month. But for three or four months, I actually made some progress. He was proud of me when he came out.

I can still run a small printing machine. I learned a lot by standing there and watching: how the machines run, how they work, what was the name of this font. I know all of that stuff.

5. When my father came to Pakistan at the time of perdition, he was very young, fifteen years old, and he came from a pretty wealthy, well-established family, because my grandfather had one of the biggest bookstores in the city. Everybody knew him and his bookstores were so big that people would come and sit, like in Borders.

At the time of perdition, my grandfather said, "I'm not going to this new country." (Laughs.)

My father said, "I'm going to go." (Laughs.) He was fifteen years old and he came alone to an absolutely new place. All he had with him were some dictionaries which he published in India, and borrowed from Grandfather. And the first thing he did when he reached the country, he sold those on the footpath and got money so he could find a place to live. Now he's chairman of the Pakistan Publishers Association and one of the most renowned business people back there.

I am proud of him. I think he did a great job. But he never spent that much time playing with me when I was young, so I missed that. I have a five year old daughter and a son and I play with them; I take them out to different places. And he never did that with me. All he did was show me the work. So I missed that part of my life, probably. But I don't know. I think he did the right thing—maybe. But I never enjoyed that part of life. (Laughs.)

Same with me, I came here not like he came; I came here with some money, but I'm pretty much a self-made man, too. And I'm in the top one percent of GM sales people in this country. (Laughs.) So that's pretty good; I'm very fortunate.

6. Courage—like how to survive. (Laughs.) You really need skills so you can survive without anybody else's help. So that's what I really picked up from him. He said, "I have been through this."

And I made it. (Laughs.)

7. (Laughs.) My father was involved in politics. And in 1971, at the time when Pakistan had war with India, he was with the political party that won the election, but they never came into power because the Army came and threw them out.

My father was an elected member. So the Army came to my house. (Laughs.) I still remember that.

They came and got my father. I was seven years old, just sitting there and watching all this with my grandmother and mother. It was scary. It was very scary. But understand that my father was pretty good. (Laughs.) He told us, "Just be calm and I'll be back in a few days." And he was. (Laughs.) And he was all right. He was an elected member; they couldn't do anything to harm him.

*8.* Now he's old and he's not as strong as I used to think, which surprises me sometimes. But I look at him now and what he was before—he's a totally different man. I thought all my life that he was very, very strong, that he had no emotions at all; but he is, he's very emotional. He cries and he does all that. Which he never did. I never saw him doing all that. All of his life from him I heard, "Do this, do that."

That's what I'd discovered about him—that he's not as hard as I thought. I think he's willing to show it now. I don't think it has anything to do with age. He cannot keep it inside now. Used to be he could, but I think he was always like this. But I never felt it that way until now. He put a curtain up there. (Laughs.)

*9.* When I was very, very young, he was not usually at home. I only saw him on Sunday; we had only one day off in that country, and sometimes on Sunday his friends came in, so he was talking to them or doing something. So, I'd hardly see him around.

I spent the most time with him when he came here to visit me. He stayed with me for six months, two years ago and six months before that. Then I really had his time because there was no one bothering him from his work or calling him; I really had a good time with him. I took him out to the Grand Canyon and we walked there for four hours. I think that was the first time I really talked to him in all my life. (Laughs.)

Other times, when he was with me, usually somebody came in or a phone call or this or that interrupted. But this time, he was listening to me.

*10.* How to survive when they are not with their kids. Sending kids away to a school, which is two thousand miles from here, or maybe even in my case, ten thousand miles, when they sent me here; it's very tough. I have to see my son every day. My wife and kids were recently on vacation without me for three weeks with my brother-in-law and I realized I have a really hard time being without my kids. That relationship has to be there because tomorrow they are going to go. (Laughs.)

I advise everybody—keep that courage in yourself. And especially in this country, it is very different. Sometimes you won't see them all year, even being in the same country. They are going to school on the East coast and you are here. Every father should have that courage.

I will try to keep them very close, but it is very hard. I will definitely send them to the schools that are good for them, for their future. I want to have my daughter around me, closer to me, and help her to be strong. My son, maybe I'll have to send him somewhere.

CHAPTER 27

# Jonathan

## *Son of Harvey, Nephew of Nick*

*1.* Jonathan, twenty-eight.

*2.* I call my father Dad or Pop; I arrived at Pop because I used to call him Poop but he asked me to stop calling him that. I call my dad, Dad. I find it very difficult to call my father by his first name.

*3.* Eighty-five percent of my friends think my father is the coolest guy in the world. A lot of my friends, when I was in high school, used to come over to my house on purpose to speak to my dad. They would arrive early so they could talk to him. One of my best friends, whose name is Shark, thinks my dad is one of the greatest guys in the world and respects him very much.

Oh, yeah.

*4.* I think the funniest story I can tell about my father teaching me a skill is when I was eight years old; I begged my father to teach me how to play guitar. My dad sat down and taught me three chords—A, D, and E. And a week later, he walked in the room and asked me how I was doing and I could play two songs for him. My dad was completely amazed at how I quickly I had learned those chords.

And I didn't pick up the guitar again until I was about fourteen.

I begged him to teach me again and he just refused because he taught me before, and I stopped. But, that is now one of my more genuine skills because of my perseverance of playing on my own and learning to be a good guitarist. Since then, he has taught me many different skills that deal with the guitar.

5. I am most proud of how my father deals with me and the way he deals with my original mother. And the older I get, the more my father treats me as an adult and as a human being. I am not the greatest person in the world, and I am not one of the easiest people in the world, but my father still treats me with respect.

6. Number one, playing guitar. Number two, is my intelligence, the way I speak and the way I speak to people, which is handy because I'm a salesman.

7. My father tried to learn to play the saxophone. My father is an excellent musician. He is a wonderful guitarist and a wonderful bass player, a hell of a drummer, and a really good banjo player. When I was about twelve years old, my father decided he wanted to learn how to play saxophone, too. When my father played saxophone, it sounded like a duck dying. So our joke was, we called it the "dead duck." Again to show how proud of my father I was, that was one of the neatest experiences, because he saw as much humor in it as I did and didn't take himself too seriously.

8. That he snores.

9. I have lots of clear memories of being with my father. But I think one of the neatest was when we visited Mom's relatives. My father and I have spent most of our lives together in the same state. And we have not ventured very far from that state.

We are from the West. It was the first time I went to the Midwest. Mom and Dad and I went to visit our extended family. And it was the first time my father and I ever saw fireflies. And it wasn't father and son any more; it was two kids, for the first time, seeing fireflies.

And that was a genuine clear moment because it was a lot of fun.

*10.* Patience. Patience. It was a fine quality that my father possessed. Because of that, it has made our relationship a whole lot stronger. And because of my father having patience, it has taught me and really made me more patient, over and over again. It really has.

And one of the greatest qualities that my grandfather, my father's father had, was patience. And he was very patient on a lot of things. When I was a child, patience was not in my vocabulary, nor would I give any body else any moment of patience.

It was very rewarding that my father had it. Some of my friends are my age and are fathers now. One of the greatest qualities that I can see in one of my buddies is that he is very patient. He has shown the utmost patience with his children since they were born.

CHAPTER 28

# Harvey

*Father of Jonathan, Brother of Nick*

*1.* Harvey, fifty-one.

*2.* Mostly Dad. And I called him Pop. Dad was what mom called him.

*3.* Dad was a quiet, bright guy with a big smile. He was devoted to his family and friends and loved Mom enough to stop drinking when she left him over it.

Mom even turned him into a hugger. I really miss his hugs.

I agree with that description, but I also remember he grew up in a world full of rejection. His mom did some really thoughtless, mean stuff.

*4.* Early on, my dad spent time teaching each of us to catch a ball. That led to playing lots of baseball. Dad became Little League manager and coach to my brother and me. It was a family affair—mom worked the food stand and our grandfathers would come to cheer. Dad continued to teach us baseball's fine points in different practices, games, and teams for many years.

Oh yeah, he also taught me not to gamble. "What do you mean you don't remember which cards? There are only fifty-two!"

*5.* Dad reached out to a lot of the kids on those baseball teams with rides, uniforms, extra practice time, food, and even money. Many of the kids really appreciated my father's attention and kindness, and they showed it. That made me very proud and aware of how lucky I really was, even then.

*6.* Dad packed our family car for a road trip like he was packing in thirty-three clowns. He told us to place all the trip items on the ground by the car. Then Dad would stand and stare at the wide-open car, and then stare at the items. This went on for a while, and I learned early on that it was a really bad time to talk or ask questions.

Suddenly he would jump into action, carefully twisting and shifting each item, trying different combinations, until all the items fit. It was packing magic.

I was a terrible packer. Each vacation I learned more by silently watching him pack. I realized later that before he started, he mentally pictured all the different ways the big items would puzzle together with the small items stuffed in between.

I eventually learned his method and now I'm the family packer. I'm good at it because I do it his way every time.

*7.* Dad sleeping in his recliner would be a family favorite and mine, too. During long family gatherings at their house, you might even catch him sneaking a little afternoon nap. And if you stayed late, you were sure to find him back in his chair. Maybe even snoring. Loudly.

*8.* When Dad died, we faced the task of moving Mom to sell the house. At one point, we started packing and emptying the storage room. As I began to remove tools, paint, screws and bolts, I noticed that the shelves were braced by narrow shims of wood. When the shelves were all empty, I realized those shims were the only supports for the large shelves full of big, heavy paint cans. I always knew Dad was not a handy guy, but those anti-gravity shelves still make me laugh.

*9.* I have many vivid memories of Dad, but I guess the clearest would be he and I golfing—we played a lot, especially in his later years. When I was a teenager he taught me how to play and he spent many years showing me how to finesse a golf shot; I still proudly use his Ping clubs. Golf with Dad gave us a four hour block to celebrate or commiserate—about our game or anything else we wanted to talk about. We had some really great talks and always had great fun golfing.

I can picture him sitting next to me in the hot golf cart as we began racing down a steep concrete path. He'd take off his hat, smile his big easy smile and say, "What a beautiful day! I love that breeze." I really miss him.

*10.* Heart. You have to love your kids with all your heart because your kids and everything else are going to pull at you in a thousand ways. And you need that kind of always on, always ready, always accepting kind of love to keep you close and on track. Heart gives you the focus and endurance to stay strong and stay together.

# CHAPTER 29

# Nick

*Brother of Harvey, Uncle of Jonathan*

*1.* Nick. Forty-nine.

*2.* It was Dad. It was always Dad. Dad.

*3.* As with anybody, it would depend on which individual was describing him and how he or she knew him. He was a good man. I've heard that, nice guy.
Oh yeah, he was a good guy.

*4.* I really don't have one, of Dad teaching me a skill. I remember tossing the ball back as a kid. But it was just tossing a ball back and I tossed the ball back more with my brother than I ever did with my father. So teaching me a skill, I don't have a real recollection.

*5.* I was proud of him that he conquered his alcoholism, maybe not some of the alcoholic tendencies, but he definitely stopped drinking. And I was proud of him for that, which I don't think I ever told him. But it was unspoken knowledge.

*6.* Oh, I think I got my alcoholism from my father. (Laughs.) Picked up his short temper. I definitely carry the mean gene—the alcoholism.

*7.* Thinking about this, it goes with question five and being proud. My wife and I had a premature child in 1993. He was three months premature and he was in the NICU for three months.

It was funny because Pop, Dad, had his business, which was a title and lien business, and it was just blocks from the hospital. It would never fail, I'd come up to the hospital at three thirty, four o'clock after work every day, and no sooner did I get up there and the nurses would say, "Well your dad just left." That happened every day. He would go up there and see his grandson every day before he went home.

And I think that's a time that really sticks with me—how he did that. It made me proud of him. He didn't need to tell people that he went up there; he just kind of snuck in, checked everything out, got the low down on the situation, and left. That really made me proud of him.

Going up to the NICU and having the nurses say your dad was just up here—that made me proud. It's a fond memory.

*8.* After he died, I found out that he was always chasing his friends, to be as successful as they were, to be as wealthy as they were. I never thought that he really concerned himself about that. So that was kind of a surprise, talking to some of his close friends and just realizing that he had the competition of wanting to be the same as his peers.

*9.* That would be when we went to buy my second set of drums. My first set of drums came from Santa Claus, and was a Japanese Lyra set which was fine, and probably built out of special Japanese wood.

But he noticed that I was a drummer and he wanted to support that. That's one thing that always I appreciated, was that even though we had very little in common, he would always support what I wanted to do; if it was art work or music work, it really didn't matter. Whatever I wanted to do, he would support.

But my fondest memory is of he and I going to purchase that set of Rogers, white pearl, drum set at Milanos Music out in Mesa. I think he was proud to be able to do that. I know I was proud to be his son because he was doing that for me. That really sticks.

*10*. Honesty. I think being honest with self and being honest with your children. As long as you have honesty, then you can work anything out. I think a father needs to have, and needs to pass on honesty to his offspring, so he can be a whole person. I think a person that lies isn't true to self. I think that's what fathers need most is honesty—with themselves and with their family.

# CHAPTER 30

# Johnny Rue

*1.* My Interview name is Johnny Rue. My real age is eighteen.

2. Dad. It was just what seemed most natural. It was what I read in little books when I was a kid.

*3.* I guess there are two sides of him. There's the business side of him. I guess he's just your ideal businessman. He does everything right. He doesn't take advantage of anybody. And everything's done the right way. He's very good at executing whatever he plans on doing.

The other side of him would probably be his family side. He's a very happy, outgoing, and encouraging person. He's very easy to talk to. He can be quite hilarious at times. He's just a great person. He's just someone you want to have in the room with you.

Yes.

*4.* I really think the most important thing he's taught me is how to deal with people. Just watching how he reacts when people get mad at him, like pointless arguments. Like with my mom, just how he handles those, and deals with those—he's very calm and he just does it the right way. He comes out on top.

He taught me how to associate with others in a way that's beneficial, how to keep my temper, and how to pick my battles. Which is very important. I have a sister that hasn't learned how to pick her battles. (Laughs.) It's funny. I'm glad I was able to learn that. She'll be a freshman next year. She'll get it.

5. I think the best example would be watching what he's done with his business. He's an accountant. He originally bought off about a hundred clients from my grandfather and used to do his work out of the house. But his clients have grown tremendously; he has about nine hundred clients now. And he no longer works in the house. He has his own office. And he even does other things. He does investments, annuities, insurance, and stuff like that.

Just seeing what he's gone through and the hard work that he's put into it and seeing the incredible pay off is something that I've admired tremendously.

6. Baseball. I love baseball. I used to play. I played about eight years when I was a kid. In high school I hurt my arm and couldn't play anymore, but I still love watching it more than any other sport.

I don't know why. It's kind of a slow moving, boring game, but I just love it. I think it's great. There's no way that could of come from anywhere else but my dad. Watching baseball pretty much goes against everything that people would see in my personality, but I do it.

7. There's one. It was pretty funny. It's actually kind of two stories tied into one.

When I was a freshman, my sister, my parents, and I went to Hawaii. Dad took my sister and me out deep-sea fishing. He caught only one fish and, of course, I caught three, including a shark. So he was a little upset. He was definitely jealous. And I remember a few years later, I guess he was determined to get me that time. Anyways, I got really seasick that time. I don't know why; I don't usually get seasick.

But I was there. I had just finished throwing up, and I was in the sleeping cabin. It was four hours into the trip, and all of a sudden we heard a ping! And the fish was on.

"All right Johnny. You got the first one," my dad said.

I ran out there. I was sick. And I hauled in this hundred pound tuna and was I proud. Immediately after, I threw up and went back to sleep. We were out there for twelve hours and not another fish was caught the entire time. And I forgot the lunch in the car, so he was really angry.

But he was really cool about it. He was really ticked off; it was really funny. He still holds that against me. I'll never get out from under that. I don't think I'll be going deep-sea fishing with him for a while. I'll let my other sibling go with him.

8. I was surprised by how much work was actually put into his business. I never saw it as anything major. But I was a kid; I was ignorant of what was going on in the office.

I actually like being there and watching him, how he deals with people and realizing what it had to have taken to get all the way to this point. I think it's amazing. It blows my mind.

9. We used to go camping all the time when I was a kid. I didn't get a little brother until I was eight. All that time growing up, it was just me and him. And he taught me a lot about the outdoors. I thought it was really special. He gave me the opportunity to have that bond with nature that most kids don't really get to experience. They just live in their houses and play their video games. But he'd take me out when I was out of school and he'd teach me how to shoot guns, and build fires, and cook stuff on fires. Good times.

10. I think they should be encouraging. I think they should encourage their kids to do good things. They should be there. They should help their kids with school. Most fathers just let their kids go off, do school, come home, show them their report card and scold them if they don't do well and praise them if they do.

I think it should be a side-by-side work together. You should help your kids. Encourage them to find a passion and go with it, even if it's something really awkward like me playing guitar. All of a sudden I came up and said, "Hey. I want a guitar."

My dad was really supportive. He said, "Great. That's awesome. That's cool. Go. Play guitar."

I thought that was amazing. I think it's very important. It helps the kids out and builds a stronger relationship.

# CHAPTER 31

# Jerry

*1.* Jerry. And I'm forty-seven.

*2.* I call him Dad. And I don't know how I arrived at that name. I am the oldest. He's always been Dad. There's been a couple of times where I called him by his first name, but that was out of anger at really bad things that he was doing at the time. But, got over that one and finally went back to calling him Dad.

*3.* They would describe him as a nice person to be around; he has a tendency to go off on tangents, and he does it very quickly. He seems to be the kind of person where he's got lots to say about everything—doesn't claim to be a know it all, but he sure has a lot to say about everything. And he will go on and on and on about whatever topic he deems himself to be an expert. I haven't heard anybody describe him as an angry sort of person because he always presents himself in a very positive way, unless it's something that's very sensitive to him.

In the last couple of years, he's gotten very sensitive over lots of things. Since my mom and he divorced sixteen years ago, he started to really get into religion more; that's really expanded a lot. I've seen him get extremely sensitive and he will burst into tears at times. You have to kind of bring him back around, back into reality.

Most people describe him as a nice guy—sometimes he's long winded. (Laughs.)

Yeah. Yeah.

*4.* Boy Scout camp—we were up at Camp Geronimo and I was trying for a wood carving merit badge or a whittling merit badge; I was trying to get a badge that had to deal with using the knife and cutting wood. I remember him sitting down and going through all the basic safety things first, to make sure everybody knew what was going on. At that time, he was teaching three or four of us all trying to work on the same thing. It was definitely, "That's my dad." He was concerned about not only me, but everybody else that was there.

It was basic safety first—know what you've got, and how to deal with the knife. He was talking about the blood circle; the circle of safety is what we called it then. If you take your knife point, and stick it out as far as you can for three hundred and sixty degrees, if anybody gets within that circle, that's where your knife either has to be folded up or be put in a safe spot. So it was very interesting watching him work with all of us. I do remember him trying to make sure that I was getting it too; so he was very concerned about his son. And he went on to talking about the requirements of the merit badge.

And then he brought out examples that he had done. He had always been a craftsman. He was surprising us with stuff that he had been working on since we had gotten there. "Take a look at this handkerchief slide; take a look at this little statue." He described how to carve it, and then had us do what he said. And then he tried to play around, and that kind of went on during the whole week.

He was checking up on how I was doing every once in a while, "It's coming along, how are you doing?" It was interesting because Dad was in his role as a scout camp leader, but he was also being my dad. So it was always understood that he had a dual role. So it wasn't like, "That's my dad and I'm embarrassed about him."

It was, "That's my dad," and there it was. When I had questions, I'd always go see him at the time to do that, and he always seemed like he knew very much what was going on. Also, it was a thing for him too, because he liked to do camping and he always wanted to be a part of this stuff. So he himself was in a different role too. So there were times when he would be out doing what he wanted to do. And he made it very clear, "I'm going to go do this and you guys can go do that." It wasn't that he was being mean; that's the way it was, and there you are.

Dad always had his own agenda. He's the last in the family, the baby of six sisters and two brothers. His brother was on the high end of the spectrum and Dad was not. And there are still times when it's very evident.

When he would try and teach me things, he was, "Okay, I'm doing this because I've got to do it so I can go back to do what I'm doing."

I would get what I was looking for most of the time, but there always was a barrier there. I remember him being very knowledge-able on the stuff that he was sure about, and he's pretty knowledge-able. But there were times when I could tell he was starting to get off track and I was like, "Okay, I've got to wait this one out."

5. This one goes back to Indian Guides, before Boy Scouts; it's very hazy. Indian Guides is a father/son thing; they get you to do things together. I can't remember an exact instance, but I do remember the two of us standing up and being recognized for something. They made a special deal about Dad. And I was think-ing, "Yeah. That's my dad."

It's the early years that I can remember being really proud of him. A little later on, it just got lost and backwards.

6. The thing that immediately comes to mind is the jewelry that he's always making. He'd go off and lock himself back in his room and he would make bolo ties and belt buckles and rings and all sorts of stuff. The thing that really stands out is I'd always get these bolo ties, prized things. It was very evident that he really wanted me to have it, and that he had given it to me for a reason.

I remember talking to him one time while he was doing lapi-dary, rock tumbling, and asking him about different rocks. For some reason I said, "Wow. This is really cool." It was an unpolished tiger-eye stone. He glommed on to that right there. I remember him describing it and where it came from.

And nothing more was said after that. Two weeks later, he came out and said, "I want you to have this."

"Oh cool." At that point in time, I was like, "Okay. Thanks." But thinking back on what he was doing, that was pretty special because he was really into the different kinds of stone and tiger-eye really stands out. He made a special effort to make the bolo tie and give it to me.

That went on for years. Every once in a while, a different bolo tie would come up. At the time was like, "Okay, great, thanks." One bolo tie was rather interesting; he had mounted a stone in the shape of the state of Arizona on some very polished steel, and right in the center, there was a tiger-eye. Tiger-eye seemed to be the theme with the gifts that I received.

7. My favorite was when Dad was three. His family had gone to the zoo, and they visited the lion cage where a lion cub had recently been born. And Dad got close enough to be able to pet it. As he turned to go, the lion cub reached out. The lion's claws caught his left leg, and took a big chunk right out of his left leg, out of his calf.

Dad went to the hospital and there were many surgeries that followed. To this day I have visions of my dad and how his leg looked; they also had to take patches from his other leg for grafting. And I think about how traumatic that must have been for him, to go through something like that at three, because kids only understand so much.

As we grew older, he would tell the story like it was no big deal for him. But you could see that did bother him, the fact that his leg was basically half of what he had originally. He also used it, I don't know if it was to his advantage, but he always would bring that up. "If I can do this the way my legs are, you certainly can do it." So okay, that gave me incentive; I can overcome adversity, too. It was just a matter of setting your mind to doing that.

Dad. Sometimes he gets very off on the wrong track. (Laughs.)

*8.* His sensitivity. No doubt. It changed after the divorce. It got more and more prominent. He didn't used to be the kind of person who wore his heart on his sleeve. He was always, "You've got to be upstanding. Take things as they are."

So as he got older and past the divorce, it was quite interesting to see how really family oriented he was. But he sure didn't show it early on. He appeared to be very self-centered in terms of his agenda and what he wanted to do, which obviously led to the divorce and all that.

Now he's sensitive about things, but he doesn't do things, doesn't take action. That surprised me. The first time I saw my dad absolutely crying was just before the divorce had gone to court.

We were having these meetings and I met Dad at the house one night while Mom conveniently went somewhere else. When I got in there, I said, "So, what's going on?" And he just fell apart, right there, and gave me a great big hug. And he was crying. I thought, man, this is really affecting him more than I thought. So it kind of changed things a little bit—made him more human.

Obviously that night in dealing with it, I said, "You guys have got to figure it out. That's between you two."

*9.* Yeah. Not a very good memory. (Laughs.) Mom was having a hard time dealing with her health, was on major amounts of prednisone, and Dad was trying to take care of things. We'd all gone to bed and I distinctly remember being woke up to a loud thud and my dad screaming at my mom, "Breathe. Hang in there, girl." I walked down the hallway to find out what was going on. She was sitting in the chair at the end of the hallway, and he was holding her up. At that point, I remember looking at my mom's face; even in the dark she was about as ashen as I've ever seen her and she was slumped over just trying to breathe.

I said, "Dad, didn't you call the hospital? We need to get some medical people out here." And I distinctly remember him just freezing. So I tried to go and get the telephone and he wouldn't let me. All my Boy Scout training was rolling through my mind; somebody's in distress and you can't do it. And here he is—he's just frozen. And he doesn't know what to do and he's running around, "We should call Dr. B.," who was our chiropractor.

I said, "Dr. B. isn't going to do any good for this." And I'm looking at Mom trying to keep her going; so some of that training did kick in; "Mom, you've go to sit up, you've got to breathe," and so on. He finally got around to calling Dr. B. and Dr. B. came over and gave her an adjustment and she did get a little better.

But it just sticks in my mind. Here's somebody I've been looking up to for all this time and when it comes down to the wire, he freezes up. It was like, gosh darn it. (Laughs.)

10. I went through this with the divorce; it comes up in many aspects. It came up a lot. Empathetic. Big time. It's easy to be strong. And it's easy to be firm, which is what a lot of fathers are. But they have to show a different side and say, "I can understand what you're saying." They don't have to be in agreement with it, but at least be willing to listen to the other person's side of the story. And be willing to deal with it, and see the other possibilities.

With my dad, it was always his way. He couldn't get that it's okay to be strong, but maybe there's another way to do this, "Can you back down, and let's try it and see if it works?"

Yeah. Empathetic.

# Chapter 32

# Stephen

*1.* My name is Stephen and I'm seventy-two years old.

*2.* I think it was mostly Dad because that is how we were brought up. We always referred to our elders, in that generation, by Dad. You never used a first name or anything like that.

*3.* Oh boy! My dad was one of those people that worked from sun up to sun down, and at night he would turn the lights on and keep working. And he always worked extra jobs to bring us up, to provide for us. He left home and started working when he was fifteen years old.

He was born and raised in a little town in New Mexico. He went to live in Los Angeles, and got a job as a maintenance man for the Bank of America. And that was during the depression when he was lucky to have a job. He met my mother there, and ironically he and my mother were both from the same little town, but they didn't know each other then. My dad knew her brother, and they met at work and got married.

I was the eldest of four kids. I remember being a little boy living in Los Angeles. I always say BF, before freeways; because that's the way it was back in 1933. I remember being a little boy and getting on a streetcar. We lived in downtown L.A., and we rode the streetcar all the way to Long Beach to spend the day at the beach; we'd take a lunch and ride on all the rides. And the whole family had a day outing for less than five bucks. Those are the kind of memories I remember about my dad.

Then we moved back to New Mexico and he worked the family farm because his older brothers had been called into the service. We lived on a small farm; we had cows, and pigs, and chickens. We had no indoor plumbing, so we had an outhouse; no indoor water, so we had a pump that pulled from the well. We grew our own food. So our basic income was what we grew, and it was a nice life. We didn't realize we were poor, except on occasion. My mother's brother worked for the railroad in New Mexico. They made a steady income and they had a nice house with heating, cooling, indoor plumbing, and all the good stuff. So we knew there was a little difference in what we were all about.

During The War, we moved to Tucson. In Tucson he worked for the railroad, which was at that time, a part-time job, so we got subsidized housing. It was the best housing we had since Los Angeles. My mother worked also for a factory in Tucson refurbishing B24s and B25s for The War.

While my dad worked for the railroad, on the side he did plumbing and construction and we built our own house. I can remember as a kid making adobe bricks. We went out with my dad in our little, old pick—up and shoveled up the kind of clay dirt and straw we needed. And every day I would come from high school and we would mix a batch of clay and straw and put it in the forms. The next day we would take those bricks out of the forms, stack them, and mix another batch. We did that until we had enough to build our house.

Then my dad was laid off at the railroad because they shut down in Tucson. So he went to San Bernardino, California, to a job there with the city in the automotive department. My brother, who is a year younger than I, went with him and became a policeman in San Bernardino. My dad retired from there.

They used to like to load up his old jeep and head down to Baja from San Diego all the way down to the point on primitive roads and in areas where there weren't any roads. And they made friends along the way; so they enjoyed their retirement. My mother had retired from the county there, and he retired from the city, so they had a nice little retirement. Not wealthy or anything like that, but just a good retirement.

Then they moved back to New Mexico and built another home over there. About this time my dad was diagnosed with ALS—Lou Gehrig's disease. Obviously that was a change in his life and in the family. He got the kind of ALS that some people get and in a year or two they are dead. He lasted eight years with it. He just withered away.

So I would describe him as a guy that everyone liked. I can only remember him giving me a little whipping one time and that was a deserved deal. He was just a good man.

*4.* I'm a pretty ambidextrous kind of guy; I can do a little bit of everything, just enough to be dangerous. But with my dad, I learned how to build. We used to make adobes. I can build a house. We used to help him do plumbing, plastering, building additions, and putting on roofs. We did general jack-of-all-trades types of things.

And that became very important in my life. When I was in high school growing up in Tucson in the 50s, there was discrimination, but you didn't know it. I went to parochial school up until high school. I already had two years of Latin before and I took another year in high school. I was an "A" student.

If you were Hispanic, Black or whatever, the counselors in Tucson at that time put you into drafting, photography, or the trades. You weren't encouraged or funneled into going to the college preps. And my folks just wanted me to finish high school. My dad had only gone to the fifth grade; my mom had graduated from high school. As we grew up, there were never people telling us we had to go to college. There was not that push from the family, and the counselors didn't give a damn; they just funneled you. But they funneled me into drafting. In the back of my mind, I wanted to be an architect. I went into mechanical drafting and then drafting houses and buildings.

And my teacher, at that point, saw my ability, so he got me a job working part time at a blueprint company. I started working at this blueprint company during the Korean Conflict. I had been there one week, when the owner got called into active duty. They told him to report in two days. His mother knew very little about the business, and with what I learned from him in one week, his mother and I ran that business.

I spent eight years with that company. After I got out of high school, I went fulltime. After eight years, I decided to go into business on my own. We only had six hundred dollars in capital and a lot of credit to rent a building, and get equipment. And going into business, I did have a partner, a fifty-fifty partner. But we didn't take anything out of the business for six months and I had no other income. We had four kids at home and my wife was a fulltime mom. That was where drafting came in.

I made more money drafting than I used to at the prior job I had running a business. In those days, I would get three or four hundred dollars for a set of house plans I could do in three nights, plus a meeting with the people. I drew a small post office branch, and small retail stores—stuff like that. The money was real good and that kept us going until we were able to draw from the business.

I learned that from my dad; the interesting part is that it carried on to our kids. We built what I call our dream house in Tucson, up in the foothills. We have three boys, and I took each one up there to work on different projects together. And they started as gofers just like I did. But now my one son can do tile, and has done tile floor additions. Together we have a house on the Verde River that we completely remodeled. My other son in Tucson had a concrete company. So it stayed in the family. We can do a little bit of everything, just enough to be constructive and do a lot of our own stuff. But it started with my dad.

5. I do remember him buying my first suit when I graduated from junior high school. I was sixteen years old. The junior high school I was in was a parochial school and it was mostly the wealthier kids in town. We lived on the south side of Tucson, and

this school was over on the north side. That is one thing I am proud of because they sent me there even though it was an economic hardship.

I had to go to junior high graduation and I needed a suit. So Dad took me down to some dinky little store and we tried on this suit; I remember it was eighteen dollars. It fit me great. I didn't know how to tie a tie; so he tied the tie for me.

There were other things that were important. He was always there. No vices. I think I saw my dad drunk once. That was funny; his two brothers came home from The War to Tucson and they said, "We are all going down to Nogales." So the whole family went down. There were the four of us kids and my mom and dad in our little '34 Ford pickup that was twelve years old.

But we went down to Nogales, and there was a restaurant we used to go to and they served all kinds of nice meals. My dad and my two uncles went off into a bar and they got plastered. It was still during The War, and we used to make runs down to Nogales because you could buy bulk meat, sugar, and coffee at half the price you could here. And so they had bought some meat and sugar and stuff. One of my uncles was so drunk while he was riding in the back of the pickup, that when they stopped at a stoplight coming into Tucson, he got out of the pickup and walked away. And it took us a couple of days to find him.

My dad was so funny. We got home ahead of him. We were kids, but we knew he was drunk. When Dad came in and sat down, his excuse was that he had a really bad cold. He was trying to camouflage it because we'd never seen him drunk before. But that was the one and only time.

6. I went into politics and I think I got that from him. He was always, tell it like it is, be a leader not a follower, and stick to your guns. He would never have done politics. But I think that if he had had a higher education, he would have gone that way. But he was content with being the patriarch and handling things from the background. My mother was a little more dominant; I think a

lot of mothers are, in ethnic communities, especially. But he'd just smile.

The funny part is, when he said something, he didn't tell you three or four times. You knew that if he had to tell you the second time, something bad was going to happen. He only had to let you know one time and it would never happen again. You just knew that he meant it. I think I picked that up from him because that is the way I raised my kids. That is probably the best trait I picked up from him. He was a good guy.

7. My dad had a sense of smell that you could never imagine. Even when he had ALS and he was immobile and all he could do was grunt and move his eyes, he still had a sense of smell. He could smell any cigarette smoke. He could smell a diesel truck two blocks away. He could smell something burning nearby. I mean he just had this terrific ability which I've inherited.

I am one of these guys that always hated smoke. I went into politics at twenty-six years old when I was first elected into City Council, and we used to have our caucus in a small room with no windows and everybody smoked but me. I would come home reeking of smoke with headaches that sometimes lasted for days. And I swore that if I ever could do something about it, I would.

I got elected in 1967 to the State Senate and one of my first items was to sponsor a bill for no smoking in restaurants. It was the first one in Arizona. I was ostracized; in those days everyone smoked. I suffered for that. I used to go back for the sessions or business meetings or to the local burger place with my family and people would intentionally light up and start blowing their smoke my way. When you got on a plane, you held your breath until you got off. Articles in the paper called me Smokey; I was called everything.

In the old days, the people who sold tobacco were the candy and tobacco people. They were the Representatives. One day this Representative who sat at the desk in front of mine at the State Senate said, "Who do you think you are?"

I said, "I'll tell you what. I'm just one person who hates smoke.

I hate what smoke does to people. I hate the smell of smoke. And I've introduced this bill and I'm going to see it through."

And he said, "Well, you'll never get anywhere with it."

And I said, "Let's see." So I was lucky that I had an ear of the senate President; I was on the opposite party, the minority party. I went to the President and said, " I need a hearing on this."

And he was a Mormon, so he said, "You got a hearing."

So we had a hearing and my secretary who had been there for many years said, "We need help on this thing."

And it happened that there was a lady that lived in Scottsdale who was leading the effort nationally for doing away with smoking on airlines. Her husband had emphysema from smoking and she called me up and said, "Do you need some help on your bill. It's wonderful what you're doing."

"Do I need help here, Ma'am? I sure do. I'm dying here."

She showed up at the hearing with about fifty little old ladies literally in tennis shoes. And the tobacco people realized they had to do something; so the hotel and restaurant people said, "If you lay off us for a year, we'll do some trials with our restaurants; we'll set up no smoking sections and all that, and see if it works."

I said, "Fine, but next year this thing's coming back." I was there for six years and I introduced it every year. I was usually the sponsor and maybe I'd get two or three non-influential people to co-sponsor with me. It really got some clout the third year because that was the year Sandra Day O'Connor went to the State Senate. And Bob Stump and Jim McNulty, both later as Congressmen, signed on with me and that gave me the clout I needed.

After six years we could get it past the Senate, but it would go to the House and die and then we'd start over the next year. Then I left the Legislature and went to Pima County Supervisor and a couple of other people picked up the bill. Two years after I left, the bill passed. I wasn't invited to the signing, even after all the time I had put in and all the crap I'd taken. I was just happy it happened.

I had that thing that drove me, that sense of smell; but from then on, it just became history. From elevators and restaurants, it just went on and snowballed. And of course, you have seen it progress to where now even whole cities and states are outlawing smoking. It took almost thirty years to get to this point, but it happened. I think it was because of the smell. I never thought about it that way.

But I got that sense from him, because my mother couldn't smell anything; she had asthma and she had one nostril that didn't work. It was funny the way he was; he was so sensitive that he could smell everything. My daughter is that way too; I think it is just the genes in the family.

*8.* I don't think there were any surprises.

*9.* This one's hard. Emotional. My dad had ALS. He was a vegetable. My mom always gave him sponge baths; she was the caretaker. I don't know how she did it, because she was only 5'6" and my dad was 6'1". I don't know how she carried him to bed and put him in.

We used to visit them once a week from Arizona to California. I went one time and said, "How long since you have had a bath, in the water?"

He said "Uhhh huhhh."

Mom said, "All I can do is sponge bathe him."

So I picked him up. Here was a 6'1" guy whose normal weight was one hundred seventy pounds, and he was down to ninety pounds. So I picked him up and carried him to the bathroom and put him in the tub. He was scared of the water; he thought he could drown, but he trusted me. I bathed him and he had a smile. He couldn't talk, but he had a smile.

*10.* Patience. You've got to have patience. Love. Patience. Leadership. You've got to be a leader in your own family because your kids need to know that they have a parent that loves them, that means what he says, and supports them. I believe those are the most important.

It works. Respect. Love. Leadership. Support.

# Chapter 33

# Blake

*1.* My name is Blake and I am twenty years old.

*2.* I called him Bruce for a very long time—that drove him insane. Around kindergarten, I started calling him Dad because my mom started calling him Dad. She had to call him Dad all the time so I would start doing it.

*3.* He's a good guy. He's always willing to help. He's a genuine, good guy.
Yeah. I like him a lot. He's a good guy.

*4.* I used to play on his Commodore 64 computer all the time. I would just trash it constantly. He would sit me down and say, "If you're going to break it, you're gonna have to do this to make it work again." So he showed me how to fix it, over and over and over again. Around sixth grade, I finally got the hang of it, and was able to do it on my own. So I stopped asking him for help; I think that drove him nuts and made him sad. The master is then outdone. (Laughs.)

*5.* Probably when he divorced his second wife. (Laughs.) He married this person and I'd have to go over there all the time. I went to my dad's house every other weekend after my parents' divorce. She had step-kids that I couldn't stand. One would throw me in the pool and I was just terrified to go over there on the weekends.

So when he finally divorced her, I didn't know about it. One weekend I went to his house expecting to be with his second wife, and instead, I went to his own place. And I was as happy as I could be. (Laughs.)

6. That would be definitely my computer skills. He taught me about the language basic, and everything I needed to know and lots other little things.

What I didn't get from him though was we rarely went outside. We went outside and played occasionally, but I accidentally got hit in the head with a bat, so we didn't play ball like most kids did.

He wasn't around much when I was in my teens, so I didn't get any type of real dating skills. So I was terrible there.

7. Probably going to scout camp. It's also one of my least favorite experiences, but it turns out it was actually so bad it was good. Man, it was terrible; I couldn't sleep. My sleeping bag was full of water all the time. I had a plastic bag around me to stay warm. It was terrible, but we were there together and it was just a God-awful time. But looking back on it, we had a really, weirdly good time.

It's hard to explain. It's one of those experiences that you just have to have. I remember walking up the hill. It rained the whole week we were there. Rain, rain, and rain—more rain than I'd seen in a long time. A bunch of us kids were going up the hill, and we were slipping and falling. At one point it started hailing; these were good size balls of hail that plonked you in the head and hurt like hell. At one point I thought, "Oh my God, I'm going to die." (Laughs.) Finally, we got to shelter.

Looking back on it, I think it's one of the best things that I have ever done because that didn't happen often. I hadn't done a lot with my dad before and scout camp was a really good time. Plus figuring out how not to die made it a good time.

*8.* When he was a kid, probably a little bit younger than me, he used to get empty buckshot and fill it with gunpowder and light it. He'd shoot them up in the sky and they'd explode.

I also found out recently that he used to go in my grandparents' kitchen and unhinge all the cupboards; his parents would find out when stuff would fall down. That's the same kind of stuff I do. It's odd how similar we are. It's like more and more things every day. "Holy crap. I'm becoming my dad!" And it scares the crap out of me.

The stuff he used to do all the time is the same kind of stuff I used to do except I used rocket engines instead of gunpowder, and I burned my hand off. But, good experience. (Laughs.)

*9.* That would probably be before kindergarten and they were still married. The most vivid thing I can remember was me jumping on the bed with my brother and Dad would throw us on the bed and bite our arms. I had these big—old bite marks on my arms. I don't know why that comes to mind, but that's probably one of the things I remember the most. Yeah, I liked it. It was fun. Okay, I did have those bite marks.

*10.* They can't be too lenient; they have to put their foot down occasionally. They need boundaries. I can see myself doing this if I had a kid, "Aw, don't do that, but oh, you're so cute, go ahead," and let them slide.

I can see myself being too lenient. My dad definitely set boundaries for me. I remember being in church and him plonking me on the head, "Hey, stop doing that. Stop screwing around."

They just have to be the enforcer of the family. So sometimes you hate him, but most of the time he's a good guy.

# CHAPTER 34

# Jay Saladay

*1.* My name's Jay Saladay and I'm fifty-three years old.

*2.* I always called him Dad. Maybe when I was a real little boy I called him Daddy. Up until the time he died, it was always Dad.

*3.* My dad was one of those generous, do anything for anybody, any time, guys. If you had a flat tire in the middle of Timbuktu and you called my dad at midnight, he'd get dressed and go get you. He was one of those guys.

He was the kind of person that would do that. He was always building something for somebody. Somebody would come over to the house and say, "Hey this is broken; can you weld this back together for me? I need you to make one of these parts. This isn't working; can you make me one of these? Can you fix the broken drawer on this dresser for me?" He was always helping others.

Yeah, I do. I grew up around scouting which teaches people to get along with others. I learned a lot of those values in scouting because scouting reinforced the values that my father would have taught us anyway. So yeah. I agree with a lot of those things that he taught me.

*4.* I would probably say that the skills that my father taught me are the skills that I use today in my professional job. I learned to weld from my dad when I was real little. I was probably nine or ten. He was working on something and he said, "Come out here and try this. Come over here and I'll teach you something. You want to learn how to do this." I got real interested in all that whether it was welding, painting or sewing something. He was a very skill-oriented person and he liked to teach other people how do those skills.

The first time you do try to weld, it looks like some pigeon flew by and deposited something on your metal. So you keep trying to weld, and after a little bit of practice and a little good, friendly guidance, soon you find out you're pretty good at it.

I guess I do the same thing with my students today. I'll tell them as we work, "Try this, do this, and readjust by doing this." A little guidance and a little direction make all the difference in the world. My father was one of those people; he was willing to give a lot of guidance and direction.

5. My father worked for Salt River Project. He was presented with one of the company's highest safety awards for longevity without an accident. Earlier, he had even helped another guy that was injured and was given a separate award for that.

Going to that presentation and seeing them give my dad his twenty-year safety award was one of the proudest moments I remember. And Salt River Project didn't give those awards out often. When my dad received his, I was really proud of him. I thought that was pretty cool to see my dad get something like that.

6. If I look back over my fifty years of learning, what I picked up from my dad most were my technical skills and the little things, whether it was in woodworking or metalworking or electrical. Those are probably the most important things that I remember getting from my dad.

I used to be terrified of electricity. Over a period of years, I now feel pretty comfortable with it. I think it was because of his training; he would explain what has to happen and that the current had to go from here to there. He told me, "You're not going to hurt yourself if you understand what's it's doing." It was the same thing with welding or painting or even if we were going hiking or fishing.

He taught me how to fly fish. When I was a kid, I thought it was pretty cool to be able to go fly fishing and tie a fly on the end of a line that actually weighed less than the line itself. And then cast this thing thirty feet and catch a fish with it; that was pretty cool. Whether technical or sporting type skills, those are the things I got most from him.

7. Our Family did a lot of camping stuff together. Our camping trip to Posey Lake up in Utah sticks out in my mind. One of the guys my dad worked with had given us directions to get to Posey Lake. It was up, up in the high forest mountains of South Eastern Utah.

So we went through Lake Powell, and past Bryce Canyon, and headed east about two hours to go way up in the mountains; the lake is up at ten thousand feet. My brother, my dad, my mom, and me were all on this trip; my brother and I were fairly young at the time.

My dad was a real adventurous sort, and going up there, he got the car stuck in the mud where the forest service was building a new campground. So we just camped where we got stuck. In the middle of the night it started raining on us, so everybody climbed in the car; my dad was the only one who got any sleep because he was sleeping behind the steering wheel. Everybody else was sliding off the wet seats. It's just a humorous story that sticks in my mind.

Next morning the forest service guys came up there and rescued us. They pulled the car out of the mud, gave us a really nice campground down by the lake, and were real apologetic about the mess. It turned out to be a great trip. On the way home, we stopped at Lake Powell and went fishing. It was just a good trip, one of the trips that stands out.

8. That's pretty tough to say. I don't really have anything that surprised me because our family was pretty open about everything.

There wasn't a whole lot that my mom and dad kept quiet. I'm sure they discussed things that I probably never knew about.

But I knew when my dad got really sick, and what was wrong with him. It wasn't one of those things where someone says, "Your dad's sick and we're not telling you what's wrong." It was all pretty much out in the open. And he made it through that.

My dad used to tell me a lot of stories about his career in the service; I would like to know a little more about that time of his life. I'm sure I'll never know about a lot of those things.

9. Probably one of my favorite memories of my dad was just after my brother had gone in the service. I had graduated high school, and my dad wanted to go fishing down in Mexico; he used to love to do that. So we loaded the car with our camping gear and my motorcycle. At Rocky Point, we headed about twenty miles south to an estuary; we unloaded the dirt bike there and I rode it those twenty miles.

My dad and I spent five days down there fishing, camping, and just hanging out. We'd get on the motorcycle together and just go exploring down the beach. That was a blast. We'd see a bunch of fish coming in by the shore chasing minnows. We'd jump off and catch fish until we were sick of catching them, and then get back on the motorcycle and ride a little farther and keep exploring. That was a really fun time. I really enjoyed doing stuff like that with my dad. That was one of my best memories of doing outdoorsy things with my dad.

10. The two words that sum up my dad would be caring and sharing. My dad cared about all kinds of things—pets, people, and the land. When we'd go camping, he'd always made us pick up litter that was lying around. I've learned a real appreciation for that. Leave it cleaner than you found it. My dad cared about a lot of things. He also worked hard to make sure that we had a lot of opportunities to do the things that either he wanted to do when he was a kid or got to do when he was a kid.

I think the sharing part of my dad was helping other people

whenever he could, whether it was starting up the Cub Scout or Boy Scout troops, or the Little League baseball program at the grade school. And he was always responding to requests of, "Fix this," or "How about designing and building me one of these." He was always helping somebody.

My dad designed a lot of things that they still use today at Salt River Project that made the job easier. He was just one of those guys that would share his ideas. He wasn't the greedy type; he'd come up with the idea, everybody would use it, and somebody else would wind up patenting it. And he'd never get a thing out of it.

I can sum my dad up in two words; caring and sharing.

# CHAPTER 35

# Jet

*1.* Jet. Fifty-six.

*2.* I called him Daddy, and that was what the siblings before me called my father and it just passed down to the younger siblings in the family. So it was traditional.

*3.* Hard working. Very stern. Self-motivated. Kind of a private person.
Pretty much, I'd agree with that.

*4.* My father was kind of like a jack-of-all-trades in the building profession. He was a carpenter. He was a mason, and a mason tender. He could do almost anything in the building field.
My father tried to teach me some carpentry, but it wasn't my cup of tea. He was a laborer for a long time. My father didn't want any of his five boys to do any labor type of work. But he did try and teach us certain things in the building trades so that we could do things on our own for our own homes. Many times I didn't pay too much attention because I wasn't interested in that; I was into school and I was into sports.
But my dad was very good in the building trades profession. He built our own house. And he built a lot of other folks' houses as well and worked on a lot of people's homes. He was very good at those skills.
My father worked a long time as a laborer, a mason tender. But

I could never figure out why because he would also work side jobs and he would lay bricks, and he would be the mason and he could do it very well. He was in the union as a mason tender and never became a regular block layer; I could never figure it out because he was very smart. He had good math skills too; he could figure out the dimensions and where the wall was supposed to be built, and how high. And he was very good at that. But I could never figure out why he didn't become a regular block layer.

He built our house from the ground up, and he could have done a better job on our house. That might have been one of his first projects because he built a couple of other homes that we owned and he did a better job on those. And then when he worked for other people, building a room or adding something on, he did a better job than what he did on our own home.

5. There were many proud moments. My mother would take us to church. From the time that we were just small kids, we were in the church. My mother was very religious. My father's mother probably took him to church as part of his upbringing, but as he raised his own family, he wasn't into the church at all. All eight of us kids were active in the church and we became baptized and we all became Christians. But my father never did then; I guess he had his reasons. I guess he wasn't too high on the Baptist preachers at that time.

But my father, when he got sick with emphysema, finally decided that he needed to come over. I'm in the Brotherhood at our church and I have been associated now for almost twenty years. I asked the Brothers from the church to come over and pray for him, and we had a meeting at my house. At that time, my mother and I had talked about him accepting the Lord. When the Brothers came over, we had our Brotherhood meeting, and my father accepted the Lord. And that was a very proud moment because he wasn't religious. He was not against us or my mother being involved in the church; he just never did go.

But that was a very proud moment, just to think that he had accepted the Lord as his personal savior. My father became very sick with that emphysema and lived another seven years after that; he finally passed away in 1991.

6. Probably more than anything else, a disciplined work ethic. My father was very disciplined about getting up, going to work, not missing work, and being there on time regardless of what the situation was.

And my father was a drinker. My father would work all week as a mason tender, which would be very rough, and he would come home on the weekends and he would drink the whole weekend. But when Monday came around, he was on the job, twenty-four seven. Never would miss. Never.

And I guess that I can say that as far as being proud, I was proud of him in many ways in what he did to take care of the family. I don't want to say we were extremely poor, but we were just a normal family. We weren't poor; we never wanted for anything. He took care of that. He was a breadwinner. He made sure that the eight children always had food on the table and always had clean clothes to wear to school. Always. He did a good job as a breadwinner; I can say that for my father.

My father was proud of his boys because we were all athletes. My father wasn't the type that would come home and express his gratitude, or tell you how good you were, or tell you had a great game or something like that. But we knew all the time that he was proud of what we were doing.

His friends would be at the barbershop downtown on the weekend and I had a game on Friday nights, so I would go to the barbershop to get money from him. And Dad would always go into his pocket and he would always come up with the money that I needed. That made me pretty proud to know that I could go up there and ask Dad for the money. And just to think about it, I knew that was a good time to go and get money because he wanted to show his friends. He told them, "Hey, I got my boys; I'm taking care of them, and here one of them is going to the game." He always had something to give; he never denied me. He would always talk about us. He was a very proud man.

7. I can reflect on one story that he was always telling people. I would go a lot of places with him. And he had an old work truck; we never had any new vehicles. And he would take me with him all the time. I'd ride with him and sit by the door. On this one occasion, we were making a turn on Broadway and my door flung open. And I was about to slide off into the street and my dad reached over and grabbed me, and pulled me back in.

And that was the story that he would tell a lot of people, "I saved that boy. I grabbed him and pulled him back in." And that was the story. I was scared to death almost, but my dad felt really good about that—he was able to save me from falling out of that truck. That was pretty significant later on in my life when I would think about it.

Pulling you back in. Many times children and even adolescents fall away and they become like the prodigal son who went out and left everything. He wanted all his money, and when he hit rock bottom, he decided to go back home and his father welcomed him with open arms. That's kind of significant, like reeling me back in from some of the things that I could have been involved in.

8. Probably his sensitivity. My father wasn't the type of father that was touchy, or told us often he loved us; he didn't seem to be very sensitive when we were growing up. He was just a hard guy.

But later on, in his old age, he became real sensitive. My father never seemed to be afraid of anything. But in his later years, when he got sick, I could see some fear.

Going back to the sensitivity, when my father was sick, and my mother was pretty sick too, I had a visit with them. I sat down and we were just talking, this was after I had become an assistant principal. And I expressed to them how much they meant to me and how much I appreciated what they did for me in helping me to achieve and get to where I was. My mother was crying and my dad, I believe he was shedding a tear or two, but he was lying in his bed. And I don't know if any of my siblings expressed what I expressed. Dad was sick, but I could tell that they both really appreciated just hearing how much I appreciated everything and that I recognized how much hard work they had done in raising the family and helping me to get to where I am.

And I just told them I could not have done it without them. And they both really appreciated that. I know my father; at that moment he had tears in his eyes as well.

9. When we were growing up and younger, my father would take me and my brother that's three years older than I on fishing trips. Almost every summer we would go up to Prescott and we would fish at Watson Lake. And we would stay the weekend—my father and my uncle, who was his best friend, and my brother and I. We had such a good time. Those were some good moments that we spent with our father. We just had a wonderful time fishing with him and doing outdoors things and he was sharing that experience with us. It was pretty regular every summer that we would do that.

And to be frank, I've taken my kids on vacations. They're all grown now, and I've done some things with them, but I've never taken my son on a fishing trip like my dad did me.

10. I would say love. Love. Caring. Being able to express your inner feelings of love and caring with the people that you do love and do care for. Some men hear that, and it's really hard for them to express love, even in our generation. It's hard for men to express love in any way to their better half or to their children. Many times my wife will say to me, "You need to show it; you need to show the love and caring. You did it when we were dating." (Laughs.) "But now you don't show it that much anymore."

Men don't like that touchy-feely type of thing, but you need to show that. Men need to break that iceberg demeanor and be able to show the love and the caring that they have for people that they do love and care for. Men need to be able to express love.

# CHAPTER 36

# James

*1.* My interview name's going to be James and I'm thirty-five.

*2.* He's always been Dad to me. Never Papa, never Pops, any of that. Always just Dad and I don't know why.

*3.* I think people would describe my father as a good listener. He's a people magnet. People like him. Somehow people feel that they are able to trust him as soon as they meet him. He's just got that effect on people.

He's a house painter. And it's so funny; he'll get contracted to paint somebody's house, and by the end of the job two weeks later, they would trust him with the keys to their house or the car or whatever. He has a way of getting trust and confidence from people. That's the one thing I really admire about him.

Yeah, yeah. He's one of the most accepting, open-minded people that I've ever met.

He's always supportive. He's the kind of person that can always find the good word. He can find the good in every situation. And that's always reassuring because when things go wrong, it's nice to know somebody who's spinning the good side of it for you.

*4.* Wow, I guess most recently was during college when he taught me how to paint. Growing up, he was a businessman, a shirt and tie man. But I think the stress of the white-collar world just wore him down, and he got sick of it. He just decided to up and start his own business. He started painting houses about fifteen years ago. And soon after that, he was taking me along, and I was working jobs with him.

He was very patient in teaching me how to cut edges and how to work windows, which is very important. When you're an exterior painter, it's very important to learn how to work windows and how to do trim. And how to do things like eliminate overspray, and keep paint off the concrete foundation. He is very meticulous. He has high standards, but he's also a very patient teacher. And when I made mistakes, he was pretty forgiving. And I made many.

One time we were working a barn out in eastern Washington. My parents are divorced; Dad lives in Spokane. But we were painting a barn out in eastern Washington, and I was mistakenly working out of two different batches of paint. At the end of the day when the paint had cured, I realized that I had painted a whole side of this huge barn out of the two different batches and that they didn't match.

He was frustrated, but he said, "Well, we'll just have to come back and do this again tomorrow." We lost a whole day over that. But, what can you do? It's all water under the bridge.

5. Oh, that's every day. I think about him all the time. I'm only able to see him about once a year. He usually comes down and stays with my brother for about a week and then he stays with us for about a week. But I haven't been home to see him lately and I kind of regret that. But, there have been a lot of times that I've been proud of my dad.

I guess when I felt proudest of him is when I was old enough to understand his trials and tribulations in the business world. My father's an alcoholic. And when I was in the sixth grade, his life basically fell apart. And he lost it. It started when he lost his job. He also had this drinking problem and pretty soon he lost everything else.

My mom had to take us out of that environment and she made a good move. There were about five years between the ages eleven and sixteen where I didn't see him. Five years. And I think that was a critical part of my development.

Luckily, after those five years, we were able to reconcile, and work toward bringing those bonds back. And I feel now that our relationship is as strong as it ever was. But it took some time, and a lot of effort. It took a lot of forgiveness on both sides. I didn't realize until a few years ago that I was just really mad at him. And I didn't know how to show that. What happened was, in 1999 I returned from Japan. I was putting my wife through college and I got a job in the import-export business in Portland. And I was doing import freight containers working for a shipping company.

It's a long story, but my father used to be an arbitrator for the PMA, the Pacific Maritime Agency. And basically, he was a negotiator between the shipping company and the longshoreman of the ILWU, the International Longshoreman's Worker Union, which is probably the strongest union on the west Coast.

And I realize now what drove him to drink, because I worked in the shipping business; it's cutthroat and it's all about money. And the longshoremen drive a hard bargain. The shipping companies are tight—I know, I worked for one.

In the fall of 2002, during the Long Shore strike on the west Coast, the Pacific Maritime Agency closed all the ports on the west Coast; ships were stacking up at anchor. They've estimated that $1.5 billion went down the drain every day that lockout was enforced. That's when I started to realize how high pressured and how high stakes my father's job was as a negotiator; because we were sitting back watching none of our freight move.

Factories were running out of parts. Perishables were being wasted. Exporters couldn't get their stuff out. And so it was rotting in the field. The whole system just came to a halt.

The PMA was the organization responsible for getting both sides to the table. This time it was ineffective; so the federal government had to step in and arbitrate to get the freight moving again. That's when I realized that he had a high-pressure job and that's probably part of what drove him to drink. And it all started making sense to me because when I was a little kid, I didn't understand stuff like that.

But I think that's when I felt proudest of my dad. I got out some of his papers and stuff from his days at the PMA and he was in on the 1971 strike as a negotiator. And that strike lasted a hundred and six days; that was a really bad one. That's when I realized, wow, he went through a lot for us. He did it for us; he did it for me.

He joined AA back in 1980 and he got sober back in eighty-four. And I think it was about eighty-five when I got to see him again. He's been sober about twenty years consecutively; he had a little relapse back in the early nineties.

6. What I've learned from him is patience and perseverance. I've seen his life go from top to bottom and back up to top again. What I've learned is you need to be resolute and if there's something you want in life, you just have to be patient. But at the same time you have to work step by step towards it.

I also think that people who do right by others, that comes back around to them. And that's something I've learned from my dad. He doesn't believe that you've got to make someone else look bad to get ahead; he's a very classy person.

7. I guess they're all fishing stories. Let me tell you the one about the German brown trout on Lost Lake. It was 1975. I was five; my brother was seven. Lost Lake is our family lake. That's where I grew up fishing—that's my home lake. We know where all the fish are. It's a nice, big lake, but if you know how the fish move, and where they are; you can just follow them around.

My brother hooked into a really nice sized German brown in front of the rockslide. That's where the lunkers hang out—the biggest trout I've ever seen. Maybe it's because I was only five, but to a five year old, that was a big fish. I guess it must have been about an eighteen incher. When you're five, it looks like a huge fish.

I remember my brother reeling it in and Mom was scrambling for the net. And that fish went under the boat; they like to do that to snap your line. He came out the other side and all I remember is those big eyes. Man, he just looked right at me. Guess what happened next? Mom was getting the net, the dog jumped in, and then the lunker went back under the other side of the boat and snapped the line. It was gone; my favorite part of the story was Dad complaining to Mom about not being quick enough on the net.

We were having a bad day, and then a few minutes later, somebody else had a fish on. Dad went to get the net and he knocked my brother's fishing rod into the water; we watched my brother's rod until it disappeared and sank to the bottom.

I've got another story; all the stories have to do with Lost Lake. We were camping down on the lake. Dad got out on a log; it was huge downed tree, about ten inches across and ten feet long. And he just sat down on it. He was kicking it, paddling himself, and drifting out. Pretty soon he was about twenty-five feet out and drifting out towards the middle of the lake.

We called out, "Dad. What's going on?"

"Oh, nothing," he said.

I think he might have been drinking at this time, might have had a beer so he wanted some privacy. Anyway, he just rode that log out to the center of the lake and he was way out there. And it was a big lake.

He was half a mile out after awhile, and we got really nervous. That's when Mom got the boat and started rowing out to him. And the dog, just like the dog always did, jumped in and swam the rest of the way out to the log to sit with Dad. Mom was mad as she pulled him in.

*8.* Well, a bad thing. I found out that Dad was a womanizer. And that broke my heart. I think that's the source of some of my anger. I was cool with the divorce until I graduated from college. And that's when I did a little independent research because that's the kind of person I am. I found that he'd been cheating on my mom. I think that's where a lot of that anger came from.

Now that I'm old enough to understand the big picture, I also realize that alcohol was involved, and I also know that he loves my mom more than he's loved anybody. He had something really good and he lost it. He knows it, and so that's his punishment. I know he's felt bad about it since.

He's very active in Alcoholics Anonymous, and he's a mentor in the program. He's got lots of friends and people that he sponsors; he's very involved in AA. He's turning his whole experience into a positive. AA is a way for him to meet people, and it's his social network.

9. It's hard to imagine not being around Dad.

I remember the trips to the beach we used to take when we were young, and just how beautiful it was. And how excited I was as a four and five year old. We'd stay up late the night before getting ready, preparing for the picnic.

I remember loading up the station wagon and getting in the car on a Saturday morning. It was only a ninety-minute drive from downtown Portland to the beach. But when you're a little kid, that's a big journey. We'd drive up through the coast range and see all the beautiful green trees. I was so excited with that anticipation as you get up through the range, "Which range is this? Is this the hill we come around and see the ocean?" I remember that and being with Dad the whole time.

I also remember when the state patrol, for doing seventy-two in a fifty-five on the way to Lincoln City, busted him! I was about five. And it was so funny because, you remember that old song? "We're so sorry, Uncle Albert." It was a joke; that was my father's song, whenever he saw somebody pulled over by the police; he'd start singing that.

"We're so sorry, Uncle Albert." And it happened to him. And so all the way to the beach we were singing that to him.

I can't remember not being with Dad in the seventies. Songs come on the radio and just instantly remind me of him and all the good times.

*10.* I have to limit myself to one? I think open-mindedness, caring. Unconditional love is what I think kids need. Unconditional love.

All I know is that when Mom had to take us away from Dad, my life got worse in certain areas, like Little League. When my parents were together, Little League was so fun because I always knew that Dad was there with his unconditional love and support. "So you didn't get any hits today, so what?" You know? But I sure missed that when he was gone.

Just support kids. Love them. And don't be so quick to judge. Because a lot of us forget what's it like to be fourteen. We shouldn't take these things personal. They're just growing up.

I just think patient, caring, and unconditionally supportive.

# CHAPTER 37

# Scott

## *Son of Fred*

*1.* My interview name is Scott. My real age is twenty-five.

*2.* I refer to him as Dad. It's always been that way, I've never known any better.

*3.* He's a very personable person. He's very good with people. Very caring, I think that he has a very big heart, and I think that definitely shows when you talk to other people and they give their opinion about him.
Very much.

*4.* I can recall my father taking us down to the park or a school for baseball, and he would hit ground balls at us all day long and it was awesome. I mean I didn't really realize how much it meant, him taking the time out of his day to do it. My brothers and I all went down there and was just a good way for all of us to be together. I think definitely I learned the majority of my baseball from my father.

*5.* I don't want to cop out behind the one that says I'm proud of him every day, but I really am. To me, he's my role model and is just an amazing person. I was there when he got athletic director of the year; and I've been there for many speeches that he's given, and awards that he's received. I've been there for all that. And I'm very proud of him in all those moments.

But I think I'm the most proud of my father when I hear other people speak of him. Because when they speak very highly of my father, that makes me very proud. And to call him my father. When people from work say, " He's the best at what he does."

Or, "He's really good; we really miss him and I wish he was back," that really makes me proud.

So I would say hearing other people speak about my father in a positive manner is definitely when I'm the most proud of him.

6. I think I got my father's competitive drive and I got my ability to want to do the best at everything; everything I ever do, I want to do the best. I see that in my father. Everything he does. Whether he's pitching pennies or whether he's the principal of a high school, he wants to be the very best. I definitely look up to that and try to emulate that.

7. At the time, it wasn't my favorite story, but now it is my favorite story by far to tell on my father.

I was in my first year of playing football. I was in the fourth grade. Anybody who's ever played football knows that initially, it's hard to get used to the contact. And for me, in fourth grade, I didn't like it. (Laughs.) I was getting killed; I'd never done this.

I remember one day, my mom was supposed to take me to practice and I told my mom, "I don't want to go. I'm done playing football. This is it. I tried it and I don't like it. I don't want to go back. Don't make me go." I was really upset, probably even crying about it so she wouldn't take me.

And she said, "You're going to wait for your father." And I just figured that would be okay. I didn't want to play. And Dad came home and we probably had one of the more serious talks I've ever had with my father in my entire life.

He said, "You don't have to play another down of football in your entire life, after this one's finished. You must finish this season.

You will finish this season. You started something; you're going to finish it. You made a commitment."

I've learned so many life lessons from that one talk with my father. Since then, I've never quit anything. I've always tried my best. I've always made the commitment to myself that if I ever start something, I am going to finish it. With the understanding that if I don't like it next year, I don't have to do it.

But I went on to really start to like the contact. I really started to like the game of football and my education was paid for because of football. And I owe every bit of that to my father.

But I hated him. I remember I hated him. He drove me to practice that day and I hated him. I didn't want to go. I didn't want to play. And I swore up and down I'd never talk to him again. And I can't thank him enough for making me keep playing.

*8.* He's over the fact of trying to impress people. I remember as a little kid I used to say, "Oh, that's dumb. Why is my dad doing that? He's silly. He's a dork." Or something, you know.

And his response to me was, "I don't care."

Usually it was at times when he was with me or my family; he's a very proud father. He's a very proud family man. His family is very important to him and sometimes he'll do silly things. He'll talk about his kids to whoever will listen. And sometimes, whether it's embarrassing or whatever I thought that he was doing as I got older, I realized that he always had the best interests of our family in mind. That realization came to me when I moved away to college. The joy he got when he came to visit or any time that I came home reminded me that he was a family man. He loves having everybody around him. When he is surrounded by his family, that's when he's his happiest. I think that's what I really discovered when I went to college.

*9.* Young. Young and camping. With my parents both in education, in the summer we would get to go camping; we really wouldn't go in the winter when it was too cold. But camping in California. We always got to go on vacation together. Going out camping, he let us shoot a shotgun. He always had the same spot picked out and we got to go fishing. Those are really clear. Those are memories that'll be with me forever.

*10.* I think the ability to keep the family, the family idea. A father can teach so much through the love that he shows with his wife and his children. I think that's it right there, the love that he can show. So often in society, you've got to be a manly man, be tough, and be hard core. For a father to put that to the side and show a soft side of love for his family but still be strong and be very secure with his manhood, I think that'll take you a long way.

# CHAPTER 38

# Fred

## *Father of Scott*

*1.* My name is Fred and I'm fifty-four.

*2.* I call him Dad. I guess when I was little, like every other kid, I called him Daddy, or Dada, and it just evolved to Dad. Thinking back on it, I've been calling him Dad since I was a young kid in elementary school. It's just always been Dad.

*3.* Intense, hard nosed, hard working. Opinionated.
Yeah, yeah they are; that's my dad.

*4.* My dad was a pharmacist. And his father was a pharmacist and his brother was a pharmacist. From a very young age, my brother and I were working in Dad's drugstores. So he taught us a lot about business, about relationships with customers, relationships with people, and about hard work. When you own your own drugstore, you work twenty four seven and that includes holidays and Christmas and anything else. At a very young age, my brother and I both learned a work ethic—what it meant to get up and go to work every single day. That's probably the biggest lesson I learned from him.

5. My dad always liked to dabble in politics. Two come to mind right off the top of my head. At one point he ran for and was elected Mayor of a small town here in north Scottsdale. And I was pretty proud of him for that, for what he did for that little community and the number of years that he was Mayor.

And also as a pharmacist, in later years, he worked for the State Board of Pharmacy. He also was a part-time teacher and test administrator down at the University of Arizona at their Pharmaceutical School. I think he was awarded an honorary Doctors' Degree and had received several awards from the National Pharmacists' Association. I'm pretty proud of that, his accomplishments, and with what he did in his profession.

6. In a kind of a roundabout way, when my brother and I were younger, we were into sports. And Dad never really saw a whole lot of value in sports. His mother passed away during the Depression when he was fifteen years old, and he grew up in a drugstore with his dad and his brother. So, of course, he didn't see a lot of value in sports.

I can remember thinking that I wanted to be at my sons' games and wanted to participate in whatever my sons wanted to do in their chosen fields of interest. So that's kind of a backwards type thing, but to me, that's something I wish he'd gotten into with me and he never did. So I learned from that relationship that I wanted to go the opposite direction.

I think I learned how I wanted my relationship to be with my kids. And I also learned his work ethic.

7. One of my favorite stories is when I was a freshman in college; we decided to go deer hunting. I went to Northern Arizona University up in Flagstaff, so my dad drove up and picked me up and we went deer hunting.

We took off up around the Grand Canyon in the woods, and we were hiking for hours and hours in the middle of nowhere. And we finally found this deer that we were going to take a shot at. I don't remember the circumstances, but the deer was too young or too little or something. We were taking aim at this deer and out of nowhere, this game and fish ranger said, "You'd better not shoot that deer." And we were like, "Where in the hell did this guy come from?"

Needless to say, we didn't shoot that deer and we kept walking. And we ended up getting lost for four or five hours before we found our way back to camp. That was a pretty funny experience. That ranger coming out of nowhere and telling us not to shoot that deer—that was pretty funny.

*8.* Just this week he surprised me a little bit. My mom and dad were divorced when I was a freshman in college, and it was not a very good divorce. They didn't speak to each other much and the split wasn't good. And that's been years and years ago.

My mom is in bad health; in fact this weekend my brother and I are going up to see her and see about assisted living for her. My dad is remarried and lives real close to where Mom is. He called me and said, "You know, your mom's having a tough time. And while you're going through this with her, she's not well enough to move to Phoenix yet, or to Texas to your sister's. She can come stay with us."

He actually went and visited her in the hospital and they had a very good conversation. And he did offer to open his home to her. And that surprised me a little bit; it's been thirty years. I was taken back a little bit, but very happy to see that. Very happy.

*9.* One is working in and being around those drug stores at a very early age. Back in those days, drugstores had soda fountains. I remember unloading boxes; our job was shipping and receiving and stocking shelves and pricing stuff. We never ran a cash register or did anything like that; we were too young. But we stocked shelves.

I have a clear memory of working with him. I also remember working my fanny off for a few hours just so I could get to the soda fountain for a coke or a vanilla shake.

I mentioned the other before, his blocking my love of sports and my wanting to do something in that area. And eventually, I wanted to be a teacher. He didn't see any value in that either. "Teachers are a dime a dozen. You need to be a pharmacist." So we had some rocky times with those decisions. He was not real happy about me becoming a teacher and certainly didn't understand the athletic aspect of it. We had some good times, but we had some rocky times.

*10.* Unconditional love for their families. Since I've had kids of my own and been married, my wife and kids mean the world to me. They tend to be the most important thing in my life. I didn't see that, at times, with my mom and dad; and I think that's unfortunate. I wish that my relationship with my parents had been a lot better, a lot closer. But you know, the kind of business he was in, he was gone a lot. I mean, he worked all the time.

I just think that you need to put your family as the central focus of your life. That's what's important to me.

The second thing would be to love them, be involved in their lives, be interested in what they do, and be part of their lives. And be there for them if they need your help.

The third would be a father has to be willing to do whatever it takes to provide for his family, going back to that work ethic thing. I've made decisions, as far as pursuing different avenues of my career, not necessarily in the best interests of what I wanted, but in the best interest of what I thought my family needed, financial and otherwise.

# CHAPTER 39

# John

*1.* John, and forty-one.

*2.* Interestingly, and my aunt says its because I grew up in the South, I still call him Daddy. Even though I hate that it sounds like JR on Dallas, I call him Daddy or Poppa.

*3.* Very grounded, intelligent, caring, good sense of humor. Very honest, very trustworthy. Somebody you could count on without a doubt.

*4.* He didn't play guitar and athletics was not my deal, but we did baseball. He taught me everything involved with that such as hitting, how to stand, and catching. He had been a first baseman in high school and college, and he was really astute at baseball.

I would have to admit, my reaction time was too slow. So I think I might have disappointed him a little bit because I never had any interest in first base. I was shorter than the rest of the kids and just couldn't move that fast, or think that fast. A first baseman needs to have a pretty decent reach, too; my dad's not particularly tall, but he managed to make up for all that. Dad coached as well and I tried various positions on the team. He always did specialty coaching. He would work with pitchers, or somebody having batting problems or whatever. So he was never the main coach. He usually did special stuff where he could work one on one with the player.

This may be kind of off the subject because I could answer just about anything that had to do with tools, baseball, shooting, electronics, and basic mechanical stuff. He taught me all those things. But I was proud of him being able to do that special coaching for me and the other kids on the baseball team. He kind of made up for those guys whose dads never had any interest in what they were doing.

I remember him showing me how to bunt. I was always afraid of getting hit by the ball. And I did get hit a few times; that started making me squeamish, even if those Little League pitches weren't that hard or that fast. Might sound counter-intuitive, but bunting allowed me to stand facing the pitcher instead of standing there with my side towards him to possibly get hit.

So I got really good at bunting. I liked the idea of getting one of the variables out of the equation. The ball has to be a variable; so let's take the variable of the bat out. And I got really good at bunting. So I looked at it as more of a defensive thing because I was fast enough to move my bat to get that ball and to take care of it. I actually got really, really good at bunting and could do things that you could only do in Little League because the other players reacted so slowly.

I was always really happy during that time because I really didn't need to work with him that much; he didn't need to show me that much because we'd practiced at home. But it was always nice that he was around if there was a problem if something wasn't working.

I remember my dad realizing that the team had one pitcher who was a hotshot but he'd get worn out, and nobody else was really very happening. But there was one kid who was really accurate but he was really slow and nobody'd give him the time of day. And my dad said, "Let's see what we can do with him." And he worked with him and worked with him. This was Dad using his smarts; what they worked out was to start the real fast, hotshot guy for the first three or four innings and have everybody get used to how fast he was throwing. Then we put in this guy that seemed like he was throwing at half-speed, and everybody was swinging early.

Nobody could hit off the guy. He would put it right over the plate each time but it would be so excruciatingly slow that batters could not make themselves wait for the ball to come over the plate. So this kid was happy because he found his place on the team, and he was actually able to do something important. Out of all the coaches, my dad was the only one to think this thing through and come up with something like that. But it was the funniest thing to see people not being able to hit off this guy that was barely letting it go.

But I feel fortunate; he's taught me so much stuff. Even with guitar, he didn't play anything but he was always interested and always backed me up. It's one of the things he used to do when I was a teenager. He would loan me money, and match me, so I could buy what I wanted. And then he would forget that I owed him the money until I started acting up; then he'd tell me he was going to remember. It's kind of funny; I'd think I'd gotten away with something, and he would say, "You better do what your mom says or I'll remember that two hundred dollars you owe me."

And I'd say, "Okay." (Laughs.) He knew what he was doing. But he wanted to help the cause.

5. Obviously there have been quite a few, but one comes to mind. I was in my twenties and had recently graduated from Devry. I was living with my parents at that time while I was looking for work in Dallas. And I did some part time stuff at the manufacturing plant where Dad was a manufacturing engineer. I helped them go through all their equipment and figure out makes, models, and serial numbers of all the spare parts they had in the place for all sorts of purposes.

And I worked with several guys who worked directly under my father and they all had nothing but praise for him. But it wasn't the kind of stuff where they were sucking up to me; I could tell that. They were saying stuff like, "This is the first job I ever had where I really felt appreciated and felt like the boss was actually taking care of us and looking out for us."

That was one where I can look back and relate it to stuff he

taught me. Knowing the way that he did things, I also knew that
he made sure his people knew they were appreciated and got them
what they needed to do what was expected of them. And he was
not the kind of guy who was trying to be in the limelight and play
games while making it difficult for people under him. I was impressed with that and very proud.

There are really quite a few things like that, but that's one that
stands out. And I know these guys weren't trying to blow smoke up
my kilt or anything like that. They had nothing to gain. It would
not have made any difference. And I could tell it was genuine. These
guys were very impressed to work for Dad. Think back to all the
people you've worked for; how many good bosses have you had?
How many could you say were great? Exactly. You could count
them all on one hand for sure.

6. Probably some annoying habits, I'm sure. Quite a bit of my
make-up in every way has come from him. It's difficult to be specific, but probably the way I tell stories, my sense of humor, and
much more. Obviously at least fifty percent of my make-up comes
from him, depending on how you look at it.

7. This one would also be about being proud of him. I was
probably fourteen and with several other guys. We were just hors-
ing around, being silly in a grocery store. And two of us, thinking
we'd be cute, shoplifted some stuff. We, of course, thought we were
real slick. We didn't care what it was; we had money, it was nothing like that. It was because we thought we were being smart asses.
Of course if we were really smart, we would have noticed the two
way glass that ran across the back wall (laughs), because we were
observed the entire time we were doing our silliness. We wound up
getting caught in the parking lot and dragged back in. I asked them
to call my father, not my mother because that would have really
been a wild situation; they did and I was very impressed.

He came straight there, and apparently told my mom before
he left that he was going to get me and that she was never to talk
about this incident. He was there lightning fast; whereas the other

guy had to wait for an excruciatingly, painful, long time. When he got there, everything was cool. They said they wouldn't press charges and we apologized and said we wouldn't do it again.

On the way home he said, "Okay, I know how this stuff goes. I'm sure that I don't need to lecture you. You're old enough to know what you did was wrong. You know it was stupid. I think now you probably appreciate why you don't want to make it a habit. I have told your mom not to ask about this and we're just not going to talk about it after we get home as long you promise me you're not going to do this again. And I'm sure I don't even have to ask you that. I think you've probably learned your lesson. This will not be brought up and that's that."

Sure enough to this day, I don't think my mom knows what went on. And if you think about it, many parents would have not remained that cool, especially with the initial phone call saying we've got your child. The initial thing would be, "Oh I can't believe this," and probably everybody in the room would know about it.

He had the wherewithal to say to himself, "Okay, this is one of those stupid things that kids do. And it's something that could be turned into a much bigger deal than it is; so we'll just call it what it is and not let it be something we're gonna dwell on. And we'll move forward."

*8.* Back in the fifties, I think he used to like to race cars a little bit. Not serious stuff, but dragging other guys on a lightly traveled highway kind of thing. Again, that's not something you'd want Mom to know about. (Laughs.) I think he used to mess with that kind of stuff. He told me he always liked the idea of having a car that was a sleeper, one that looked like something your mother would drive but had a serious engine in it so he was able to smoke somebody on the way home.

*9.* I can think of lots, but this one pops in my head. Going back to when I was much younger, he needed to do something on a Saturday at the manufacturing plant that he was engineer over. It was in a smaller town outside of a larger small town (Laughs), if you will. And I remember going there with a shotgun; I don't remember if it was his father's shotgun or some other thing he had. And I was fascinated that we drove there together.

And then he went in, and came out to check on me periodically. I walked down a slope to where there was a creek. The plant was so far out in the sticks that it was okay to for me to play around out there and shoot at stuff while he was inside doing his work. And he'd come out and shoot a little bit, and go back in and do some more work.

And then there was the excitement of just hopping in the truck and driving back home like everybody can go and do stuff at their dad's work. I think back at that and don't believe it.

Just that general feeling comes to mind. His liking to go do things, whatever they were, whatever I was into at the time. He liked to be part of it, whatever it was.

I feel very fortunate, especially now that we actually talk about this stuff, about all the guys who's dad ran off on them when they were kids, or beat them, or whatever. It's nice to be on the opposite end of the spectrum.

10. I would say the one that I alluded to before with the harmless shoplifting thing. (Laughs.) The ability to be cool when something that doesn't seem so good happens is probably the most important, to collect their thoughts and see what's going on and not be reactionary. And say, "Okay, stuff happens; let's see what the facts are and see what it's going to take to fix this," and not be emotional and fly off the handle or worry.

Like in my shoplifting case, Dad wasn't worried about what the neighbors would think or anything like that. Of course he might have been, in that we were going to consider this a done deal and move on and not talk about it. But the fact was that he didn't seem like he was thinking about potential embarrassment. He just took it for what it was, and kept it isolated and didn't let it blow up into a big, stupid, deal.

People expect a father to be able to field whatever life throws at them, along with so many other characteristics. Obviously, we're older now and we know life is not that simple. But as a kid, you expect Dad to take whatever happens, rationally deal with it, not freak out, and not do things for the wrong reasons.

CHAPTER 40

# Killbird

*1.* Killbird, forty-six.

*2.* I call my father Pops. Pops is one of those names that I guess was just given; I just gave it to him. It was different. Daddy sounds kind of gay-like and Pops just sounds—it's got a punch.

*3.* Well you figure coming up, he used to drink a lot. So to me, there wasn't any describing him. He never talked a lot. He's a quiet, honest, fair man. Real quiet. When the alcohol took it from him, he didn't have anything else to say. So he was quiet, real quiet.
Yeah, yes.

*4.* You figure over half the houses that we had coming up, there was always something wrong. I was the second oldest; my oldest was a brother too. But whenever there was something needed to be done as far as fixing, I always got called to do it. So Dad taught me how to do a lot of stuff around the house—lots. Plumbing, electrical, I had to be the one to read the directions; Dad wasn't much of a reader, so I got taught that early. So today when anything goes wrong at my house, I fix it. I also take care of my mother's house. It definitely paid off. Big time.

*5.* Had to been graduation night; for a man that didn't talk much, looks did a lot too. I brought home my first "F" my senior year. The look I got from him for that "F". I got an "F" that first semester; so my second semester I had to take two English classes back to back and I got an "A" in both. And that just made his day. So I did my part and he did his, without much words.

*6. Dominos.* Coming up, he was a bad actor; he figured he could beat everybody. So it got to the point when we were old enough to count the numbers, that we were his sparring partners. He and I sparred long enough that it got to the point where I was the baddest. So, I got him back. He won't play me any more. So dominos was it.

The guy I am talking about right now, I consider him my daddy. My biological father wasn't around when I was growing up. It's funny, I can remember back to when I was five, and my stepfather's been there.

I also remember my biological father coming by when I was maybe six or seven with toys and stuff. I said to him, "Yeah, you're my daddy but you ain't been here." And I tore all that stuff up right there in front of him.

And he tried to get me and my stepfather said, "No you're not." So that was another time I was proud of my stepfather, my real father. My stepfather has been there since I was five; that's my daddy.

*7.* When we were like ten or eleven, he used to golf when we first came to Wichita. My brother and sister and I stayed with our grandparents until we were about ten when my grandmother passed away and my mother and he came and got us. He wasn't an avid golfer, but he went golfing a lot. He had a couple of White friends that he golfed with; so my brother and I had to be the caddies.

We were on the golf course once and we were all walking, and my brother happened to get behind me. We walked on for about fifty yards, and I looked around and I said, "Where's my brother?" And we all went looking everywhere and we found a hole in the golf course that my brother had fallen in. I guess it used to be a well or something. My father was like Superman, and got him out.

We could have lost him because he just fell down in the hole. We looked all over, and there wasn't any sign about a well or a hole.

*8.* During his teenage years, Pops' brother got killed; I think Pops was thirteen. Like I said, with him not really being a talker, I never knew how he could hold that in. I think I would have lost it had I lost my brother at an early age. But he maintained well as far as I could see. That would have to be it, him losing his brother.

*9.* I got a clear moment. He drank so much, especially on paydays. I remember at the early age of eleven, getting out of school, and I was with him. He used to always have three speed on the column trucks. That day he was drinking and he drank too much. And I said, "How we gonna get home now?"

And he said. "You're gonna take us." I learned how to drive that day and we made it home. But I'm almost certain I had been driving in his lap before that, even shifting the gears. I rode first gear for a while, and he woke up and said, "You need to shift gears." So I learned how to drive real young, a stick even. I think today that my sister and me are the only ones that know how to drive a five speed.

There was a lot of that once I learned how to do it. Man, I'd get out of school on Friday, he'd say, "You're going with me!" Okay, I was the designated driver; back then it wasn't what you called them. But yeah, I learned early.

*10.* Be a father, because like they say, anybody can have sex. If you're going to help make the child, then you have to help rear the child too. I think every father has got to have that responsibility. If you just go around making babies, you really did nothing; you're not a daddy. A daddy, a father, a confidant, is somebody you can go to when you can't go to anybody else. So be that person; be a role model.

I can honestly say this about my father, my Pops. Hard as he was, I have not once spent the night in a jail. And I've got to say he's the reason because of the consequences; I've got to give that to him. And God. Or God and him. But I know that it was for him. I never spent the night. And I wasn't going to repeat anything, either. (Laughs.) Just going, that's trouble; that's trouble big time. So, I've got to credit him with that. Like I said, I've been, but I've never spent the night.

# CHAPTER 41

# Raphael

*1.* Raphael, fifty-three.

2. Dad. Just always Dad. Never Daddio.

*3.* Meek, mild, well mannered, non-confrontational.
I guess that's me saying that's what he is. I guess I've always seen him like that.

*4.* When I was in Cub Scouts, I had to make something, and it was a kerchief knot. And we didn't have any tools. Just little bitty hand tools, nothing significant. He was a maintenance welder in the oil refineries and steel mills back in the Mid-West, and he never had any tools at home—pliers, screwdriver, hack saw, coping saw.

We had some scrap wood lying around and he had some chisels that were wood carving tools that I never saw him use. But they were a really precise, intricate, very tiny set of hand tools. He virtually made the kerchief knot, and we both painted it with house paint. But it was this knot, a wooden disk, with a Navy anchor on it because he was in the Navy and it was just a block of wood in the back with holes drilled in it for slipping the kerchief which he had done with an auger drill bit and a strange drill. Crude, but it was fun just watching him work and seeing him have that excitement in having a plan and doing something.

5. When I was fifteen, my parents separated. It was because my mother was having another affair or a current affair; this was the first we'd ever known of. She asked my father for a divorce, and he left. About eight months later as my mother was being evicted from the house, we moved to another place and my father moved back in with us, and my mother continued another affair.

She worked tending bar late at night, and she would come home late. And one night she came home and went to bed—the first time in my life I'd ever seen them sleep together in that house. They had been in bed for about an hour when the phone rang and she answered it. And she talked for over an hour, lying there in bed, right next to my father. She was laughing and joking, and when she got off the phone, he asked, "Who was it?"

"It's none of your business," she said. Then she said it was her boss. Then they started arguing. And he proceeded to beat her with the phone; it was the first time I ever saw him raise a hand to her. And the first time I ever saw him stand up to her.

And then he proceeded to leave and I was cheering him on; oh boy. Not because he took out his frustrations on a woman, or beat a woman up, because I would never consider that as an option, but because of the fact that he finally stood up to her and I was of proud of him.

Weeks after the episode of my father hitting my mother, and after she had filed for divorce, I was eating dinner with my father at a greasy spoon a few blocks from our house. And he started crying. He just sobbed deeply.

As I look back through my life, I was so proud of him because he was able to share that with me and be able to have that depth of emotion, to share it with me and not hide it. I know a lot of men who would think of that as being weak, but I believe it is the most wonderful strength to show that vulnerability. There's no weakness in sharing.

6. I have his walk. He used to work evening shift, and my brother and I had our bedrooms in the basement. I was nine years old and when I would go to bed at night, every creak in the house

would keep me absolutely petrified thinking that somebody was coming after me.

I would hear him come home at night and I would be awake and waiting because if I wasn't, somebody was going to get me. I'd hear his key in the door and even that startled me, but it kept me alert as I listened to him walk across the floor. I knew it was him. He was home. And I knew I was safe. And before he got downstairs, I'd be asleep. Because I could rest. My mind was at ease.

So I have his walk. I pride myself. Everybody is in such a hurry to get some place. But when I walk, it's like I'm walking in his shoes. I'm walking his pace, his cadence. He gave that to me.

7. When he died, I was a student at ASU and I was in the process of completing two different classes of sculpture. In one of them I was creating a piece of sculpture that involved something that the instructor named "new directions"; we were documenting what you would call the human condition. Yet being akin to kinetic sculpture, it would involve movement or implied movement. And so he said to watch life cycles of plants or animals. He said, "If you don't have one, get a pet, or buy a plant."

I had seen photo displays and exhibitions where artists would take a picture of themselves every day for the course of a year, first thing in the morning, every day, same time. And then document what they look like and then show them altogether in one exhibition. And you could see them hung over, sick, just laid, or up all night. So I thought, "I can do that," and I decided to cast my face on a daily basis to document the growth of my beard. On the twentieth day, my father passed away.

And so I couldn't cast my own face; so I went to the funeral home to cast his. And my sisters were okay with it and my brother was out of the country; coincidentally enough, he was in the Philippines with the military. So my sisters said okay and my brother-in-law said, "That's Raphael. He's just crazy. You know him."

I approached the mortician, and he said, "You can cast the face under one condition; you have to let us watch and tell us what you're doing because it's so exciting."

I took enough material to do two castings in the event that I made a mess out of the first one; an emotional upheaval might require scrapping the first one to start over. And as I talked my way through it, it was like I was able to remove myself from the emotion of the process. I was able to stay so focused on what I was doing and take such care, even though he was dead. I didn't have to put straws in his nose, of course, which I would have had to done with myself. But I was almost like, "I forgot the straws!" And of course, I didn't need them.

And I made a plaster positive out of the cast. Then brought it home and made a bronze mask to incorporate into the sculpture with the other thirty masks of mine. The sculpture is each of the masks mounted on three-eighths inch stainless rods. My father's mask is at eighteen inches in the middle of an infinity loop. The first twenty days of mine start out from his mask and go up to eight feet and then come back down where all the masks are facing out away from him, as if I were moving out from my point of origin, kind of like the big bang. It's all these different aspects of me, different character traits, coming from my point of origin.

The last ten days are after the funeral, and go up into another loop about six feet tall and come back down to the last day. On the last day, I have a clean shaved face and my mask is looking in on him as I last saw him, which was in his casket. All of my masks are in plaster. His is in bronze.

My siblings have to go to the cemetery to visit Dad and he's in my living room. All the other masks of mine are put away, but Dad's mask is in my living room. I see him every day. He's always there with me. And he is. He's always there. Whether it's in the bronze or just being present with me, but he's always there.

I always thought as a maintenance welder in a steel mill, other than his children and his grandchildren, Dad left nothing behind to show that he ever existed; there may be a file somewhere in the Navy archives because he served in World War II. But thousands of years from now, somebody will dig up this bronze at the bottom of a canyon somewhere in this state and wonder what person was powerful or important enough to have a death mask made of him.

*8.* During his convalescence from his heart attack and his recovery from emphysema, Dad had to have oxygen with him all the time. My mother had talked him into being incapacitated and an invalid, so he was pretty much at her mercy. And I think she really enjoyed making him an invalid. A lot of couples do that to one another.

But then she became incapacitated. He had let his driver's license lapse and couldn't drive to see her when she was in the hospital. And I said, "You've got to."

He was seventy years old and he said, "I can't."

I said, "Why not?"

"Because I've got this oxygen bottle. How can I drive?" he said.

"You put an extra long cord on it and you stick it in the back seat," I said.

"But, how am I supposed to drive?" he said.

"You get the book, study it, and take the test." And he did. And he was so happy to see that he could do that for himself. And he realized he wasn't an invalid, and that somebody had to be in control. With my mother having her foot removed, especially her right foot, she wasn't going to be able to drive. And if they were going to survive, he had to drive. He got his power back. I was surprised to see him so joyful that he could do something that he thought he wasn't capable of.

*9.* In 1978, his emphysema collapsed one lung and he had suffered congestive heart failure. He was put in the hospital's cardiac unit. Dad was a very private man, very meek. I never saw him naked, except maybe in the shower, and he would hide behind a washcloth if we came in to go to the bathroom. I never saw his private parts, his genitalia, ever; whereas, my mother would walk around the house half-naked or scantily clad most of the time.

He didn't have the strength to clean himself, but he was so proud and so private that he couldn't ask the nurses to clean him either. My mother said, "Help your dad. He needs you to help him." He couldn't even ask her to do it; he was so private. And at the time, I was a nursing assistant orderly at the hospital. So this was no accident.

I was trained to be of assistance to people when they are at their most incapacitated. How could I not help my father at this time? He had a catheter, and he was really encrusted with a lot of dead skin, and just a mess down there. I don't know how I knew what to do, but I used Vaseline Intensive Care Lotion and just slathered it on the area. Then I cleaned him intricately with the washcloths, as if I were taking care of myself, or any patient that I had.

And yet, he wasn't ashamed. He wasn't embarrassed. And it wasn't anything other than just his discomfort and his needing to find some relief.

He had a catheter, he had IVs in both arms, and he was unable to do anything for himself. And I know that he had wiped and washed my butt many, many times. And it was kind of like a payment, a return, and a full circle. And I was proud to be able to help him, and do that for him. None of my other siblings could have done anything like that. It was just like I was in that place, in that position, just so I would be able to help him.

*10.* One thing I see so much in our world is that men can teach their children their masculine traits but they don't embrace their feminine side. I believe that we are a combination of male and female and that too many men never touch on or embrace the feminine. But they need to acknowledge it so they'll have better relationships and have a better connection with women. And I think it's up to the fathers to teach that because I don't believe they've been taught themselves. But it's about learning it, and knowing that it's a part of us that is always there, and not denying it, or turning it away; it's about our intuition.

When my father showed me his ability to cry, he touched on that. I don't think he ever came out verbally and told me about it. Yet, for me, that was just the tip of the iceberg, the beginning of being in touch. Other than that, I can't say that I really had a whole lot of respect for my father because we didn't have much of a relationship. He worked, and when he wasn't working, he was passed out. He'd stop after work and have a few beers, and when he got home he was dead tired and would fall asleep as we ran wild in the house. It wasn't like we had a lot of time together. I had more of a relationship with him when I got older.

CHAPTER 42

# Teddy

*1.* Teddy, seventy-three.

*2.* Dad, because I don't really remember what I called him when I was a child, but he lived to be eighty-two years old and we were very close at the time that he died. So it was always Dad.

*3.* I think that depends on who's doing the description. My father was a self-made man, and he could be very cantankerous, and strident. Or he could be very kind; he did a lot of charity work. If you went through a broad sampling of his acquaintances, you'd find people who would not be complementary, and you would find people that think he was one of the more unusual and most talented people they had met. And also he had a very kind heart. He did a lot of nice things for a lot of people.

*4.* He was an excellent woodworker. He taught industrial arts in high school for many years. He even made a lot of the better pieces of furniture that we had in our home during The Depression.

What comes to mind is he helped me make a birdhouse when I was a Cub Scout living in Ohio. He showed me how to put it together and so on, and probably helped me more than I helped myself, and the birdhouse won a prize in the contest.

*5.* My mother and father had some very dear friends who were of their same age or perhaps a little older. And these friends had little or no money; they lived on social security and a pension. They both outlived my mother, and as they got older, their needs went well beyond their income and my dad bought them a house they could live in on the west side of town. And he would see that there was always some food on the table for them. He did that for years.

After he died, I inherited that house and I did what he did. I took them over; they stayed there until they both died. That's one of the things that comes to mind.

6. I have some of the personality traits of my father; at least my wife feels I do. She feels I can be a little more blunt than I should be sometimes, and that was a characteristic my father had. He wasn't a diplomat; he didn't mince words with people. If he liked them, he was kind to them; and if he didn't, he was not particularly civil. I suppose that's a genetic trait.

Honesty. Going back to my childhood, one time I broke out of the house when I was three, very young. I went downtown and got in the dime store and helped myself to a little car and a Big Little Book and made a general mess. They got a call that the three year old was running around downtown, so my dad had to drop everything at his workplace and come get me. And I remember he put the little car and the Big Little Book up on the hearth of our fireplace, and he gave me a paddling. And he told me I was never, ever to take anything of anybody else's without paying for it. And that stuck. And I think that's probably one of the big things that he did for me.

7. My father was a very ambitious guy. He grew up on a farm during the twenties, and he went to Ohio State and worked his way through college. And in the summers he would go back to the farm. There was an amusement park not far from their home, forty or fifty miles, called Indian Lake. It had a full roller coaster, merry-go-round and all kinds of little stores.

People would come to the lake and rent cabins and then they would go the amusement park. And Dad had two booths there.

And he hired one of my uncles to run the watermelon booth; he would go to my grandfather's farm, bring the watermelons in, put them under ice, and sell watermelons. And in another booth were potato chips. The potato chip booth was very popular; Dad would sell them in bags or five-gallon cans.

My mother went to Indian Lake with a bunch of girls. They were walking down the causeway and my mother saw my father cooking the potato chips and thought he was cute. So they agreed to buy a five-gallon tin of potato chips, which was a big order, if he promised to deliver them that evening to where she was staying. And that's how they met.

They dated for the three days she was there. She was from a town fifty miles from his dad's farm, and before ten days had gone by, he proposed marriage. They got married the next January. So he was a man of quick decisions.

*8.* My mother died in 1968, which was quite early in her life. And I was surprised when my father, within less than a year, got remarried. And probably, I gleaned from the circumstances that there had been some kind of relationship between the two of them prior to my mother's death, but I was never involved in that. That surprised me, that after thirty-six years of marriage, he didn't mourn more. He immediately went back to the well, if that's what he did, and married this other woman. Which all worked out all right, although she ended up divorcing him later.

I was surprised because of the stability of our home up to that time. My father was in the finance business and was a manager of a finance company in Ohio, which was a good job right in the middle of The Depression. In 1940, my mother got very sick with tuberculosis. And the doctor finally came down to that fact and said; "We can't do anything for her here. The only thing I can suggest is to take her to Arizona, to a dry climate. People go there all the time. Maybe, she might recoup."

So my father, right then, no decision said, "We're going to go to Arizona." He got train tickets and took her out on the train. The doctor told him that he didn't think she would make the full journey, but if she did, he had a hospital, Good Samaritan, for her to stay in, and a doctor for her to see. The doctor's son, by the way, later became my law partner. My mother spent seven years in a sanitarium here and became well.

After he came back from Arizona, having taken my mother out there, he sold everything we had except a Dodge car and a really nice trailer he made himself because he was heavy into industrial arts. He got seven hundred dollars for the piano and the furniture. And we moved to Arizona with a Dodge car and seven hundred dollars.

That's the kind of guy he was, that was the stability, and the love and devotion between the two of them that I was accustomed to. So I guess that's the surprise, the quick remarriage. Whatever happened, he dealt with it. And dealt with it quickly.

*9.* We used to deer hunt after my mother had recovered; that was just before I went in the service while I was in college. We liked to deer hunt together. And I think that those trips deer hunting were very special because we would go out and do something that was so different from what we usually did and we would go for a longer period of time.

I got to spend seven to ten days with him, and sometimes we would take friends. But it was a camaraderie that we never really had while I was growing up, because while I was growing up, my mother was ill and not at home. My dad and I did the cooking. He worked, sometimes two jobs, a full day. So we didn't have a lot of close time when I was a younger man. So deer hunting was very important.

*10.* I'm very opinionated about that. I don't think a father ought to bring a child into this world without seeing that child through his education, regardless of the marital circumstances. And certainly my father typified that.

But I think it's a lack of that characteristic or pattern of responsibility for your children, whether they're conceived in wedlock or not, that has been the ruination of our modern culture, particularly

in the Black communities. People don't grow up well in a one parent environment. And I'm always very disappointed in any man
who will not see to his family duties and to his children. And that
doesn't just go with idea of supporting them financially, but it has
to do with raising them, and giving them character, and substance
for all of their life.

# CHAPTER 43

# John Smith

## *Son of Dave, Grandson of Randolph*

*1.* John Smith, twenty-five.

2. I call him Dad just because that's what I've called him ever since I can remember.

*3.* Hard working and dedicated. Dedicated to what he likes to do.
Definitely.

*4.* I always have to go back to when he taught me how to play the drums. He was the one that bought me my first drum set. He's the one that always got me motivated with music. That's my fondest, and the one that I still use the most today.

*5.* I got a ticket for littering, and he represented me as my lawyer in court one day. I was more than proud of him for getting them to cut my fine down by half.

*6.* It has to be the love of music. I can't pin down anybody else that has turned me on to music as far back as he has.

*7.* When we used to live back in Claremont, he and I used to take the dog up to my old elementary school. I remember the look on his face. He had just thrown the ball for the dog. I was four feet high and the dog came running at me and he took my legs out from under me. And I cracked the back of my head on the black-top. I just remember Dad coming up and shaking me to see if I was all right because he thought I was out. That one always makes me smile.

*8.* How much he and I are exactly the same. It makes me laugh; I'll put it that way. The way we go about things, and the way we think about things is almost identical.

*9.* I remember him taking me fishing up at Big Bear. This was after he and my mom divorced. It was just me and him going fishing and camping out in Big Bear. That was a good memory that I think about a lot. He was definitely the one who put a fishing pole in my hand and showed me what fishing was all about.

*10.* I think the fact that he has been stern and up front with me since I was real little makes me appreciate him more now. He's kept me out of trouble; I'll put it that way. And it's the way that he's taught me to go about things, as far as what's right and what's wrong. His way of how to go about things and deal with stuff has paid off in dividends.

# CHAPTER 44

# Dave

*Father of John Smith, Son of Randolph*

*1.* Dave. I'm still fifty.

*2.* To his face I call him Pops, Dad, or Father—a variety of names. But I will use his proper name when I refer to him with most everybody else.

*3.* The people that knew him knew him through his work, and I think people would say he was a go-to-guy. He was the guy that got it done. He was the go-to-guy; that's how I think they would describe him.
Yeah.

*4.* It wasn't patience for sure. (Laughs.) The skill I would say he taught me might have been tact. It might have been how to read people. He was good at that.

*5.* I was in high school when my grandmother got run down in the alley by the Bow and Arrow Brothers on a bicycle. They knocked her over and broke her hip. She was a big woman, and my brother and I somehow got her in the house. And we called our father on the phone and he came home. We didn't know how to get her where she needed to go, to the hospital or whatever.

He came home and he picked her up. He carried her down the stairs out to the car, put her in the car, and got her to the doctor. They got her x-rayed, and did whatever was needed. But more than him just picking her up, which was amazing to me, was that he was the guy. He took care of it. And I recall being proud of him for that.

6. An amazing lack of patience, yes.

I will credit my father with this; I think I got an ability to get along with pretty much anyone from my father. Because I see that as something he was able to do.

7. I can't think of one at this particular time.

8. When we were older kids, we learned that he was a card player; Dad used to play cards. And he was good at it. They called him Diamond Jim because he always beat everyone at cards. He'd take everyone's money.

We didn't play cards with him growing up. He was not a gambler with the family; he was not a gambler at all. That was the surprise because he wasn't a gambler, certainly not with money and that kind of stuff. So to learn that he was a card shark and was referred to as such by his friends in college and in the military, yeah that was a surprise.

9. This is a rather easy one, but it's too easy in one sense. As my brother and I grew up, there were very few times when there was a lot of closeness between our father and us, physical or otherwise. I don't recall him being close. It's not that he wasn't interested; he spent a lot of time working. So the times that I would recall being with my father would be the obvious vacation times.

At one point in early high school, we went to the Grand Canyon and rode those stinking burros down the long, fucking trail to the bottom of the canyon. He and I spent the night down there and did the reverse coming back. That was a good time for us. He enjoyed my company, and I made him laugh. I can make him laugh. And we had a stress free, good time.

*10.* Responsibility comes to mind. That's the only thing, and that's the main thing a father's got to have—responsibility for their kids. If you're not a father, you almost can be irresponsible in some measure for yourself, your spouse, or the rest of your family; but for your kids, you have to be responsible. You've got to be there to take care of business. And that goes beyond just going to work and making money.

The duty of a father is to be there, step up, and be responsible. That's part and parcel of loving your kids. But even if you don't love your kids, you've still got to be responsible, which most fathers certainly do. And even if there was some reason you couldn't develop love, or if you didn't like your kid, you've still got to be a real father.

Those two words are synonymous. Being a father is being responsible.

# CHAPTER 45

# Randolph

*Father of Dave, Grandfather of John Smith*

*1.* My name is Randolph and I am eighty years of age.

*2.* I called my father Dad. I have no particular recollection of why it was Dad versus Pop or anything else.

*3.* Probably in a positive fashion. I think they would say he was tough—strong willed and tough, and probably demanding.
Yes.

*4.* My dad had little time to play when I was of the age that fathers played with their offspring. If he taught me a skill, I'm not sure what it would be; maybe it was when I got my first bike and he helped me learn to ride it. I'm not sure there's much more than that.

*5.* There was a certain amount of pride when he explained to me why and when he left his position as a senior executive officer for Kaiser Steel. I was twenty-two, back from the service, and going to college. I never quite understood why he walked away from an important position with a very good salary; I remember being quite buffaloed, and baffled. And when he explained the whole situation and background to me, I had to say that it took a lot of guts on his part to leave that job.

When I was going to Claremont Men's College, I commuted from home. My dad was working as a Deputy Sheriff for Sunkist growers, a few blocks from their home. My dad owned a Studebaker Champion that he bought new, prior to The War. I commuted to Claremont from Ontario in that Studebaker Champion.

One evening, when we college students were carousing on Foothill in the wee hours of the morning, I took out most of the brush in the center divider and totaled that Studebaker Champion. I managed to get it home and parked it in the driveway.

To the day my father died, he never once asked me what happened, or how it happened, or anything. He looked at the car, and obviously saw it was a complete wreck, so he traded it in and bought a new car.

Never once asked me about it.

6. I may have developed a work ethic that was the result of something I got from my father. He worked hard and he played hard. He was also honest. He demanded a lot, but he was willing to give a lot.

7. My dad could tell stories and jokes with the best of them. Somebody would come up with a story, and he had one in response.

I recall in particular being up on my grandfather's farm on a Sunday afternoon, with my dad and a number of my uncles. They jacked up the rear wheels of the Ford and attached a five-gallon ice cream maker to the rear wheel. And they sat there and sipped whisky and told jokes while the ice cream was being made. They made two freezers of ice cream that day. I can remember the good time that they had and my father was in the middle of all that.

8. My dad passed away when he was eighty-one. In the last few years of his life, his vision had gotten to the point where he was almost legally blind. My wife and I recognized that he could not see

well. It came to a point where he felt he no longer could drive or should drive, and he gave up his car to a grandniece. He recognized it, as did my mother; that was pretty astute on their part.

9. My dad was a generous host. On one occasion after we were married, he took me and my wife and Don and his wife to dinner down at La Soranas Country Club, south of Pomona. He was a good host; he liked to party. He played hard. He drank hard.

10. They should be honest and they should be up front with everyone, especially their offspring. They should be a devoted and dedicated parent. Any father, any parent, should be a good listener. They should listen more than they speak. I suspect that if my dad had a weakness, it was that he didn't listen nearly as well as he could or should have.

# CHAPTER 46

# Joshua

*1.* Joshua. Age forty-six.

*2.* Dad. It was mainly a very simple and easy way to communicate with him. We actually transitioned from Tata, which is more of the Spanish version. So as we became more fluent with English, we changed it to Dad. Tata was the first, and still is, especially when we are in a setting where people are predominately speaking Spanish.

*3.* He is the most non-traditional Mexican male that you would ever meet. He would cook eighty percent of the time, and would do the dishes eighty percent of the time. He would not go out and drink and hang out with friends. He just embodied the most opposite image of what a person would typically think of as a macho Mexican or Hispanic person. He is very easy going and very patient.

But when it came to discipline, he really had a very strong standard that he set for all of us. And his approach was more of the old style in terms of his discipline with the kids, and yet at the same time, more for the boys than for the girls. He tended to be a little softer with the girls.

There were times when he put on the role as the typical Mexican male when friends would come over. He was certainly out of the kitchen and my mom and the other females would do all the cooking. They would always serve the males first, then the males would sit around and drink and talk, or whatever.

Outside of those episodes, he was a very non-traditional Mexican male.

Absolutely. Yes.

*4.* There were two things; one was hunting. He did lot of deer hunting. We came from Mexico when I was almost seven. As we got a little bit older, he would take us out hunting, and I was the oldest boy. And we went to the rifle range, learned how to sight using the scope, and did target shooting. And then we went out and actually did the hunting, the spotting of the deer, and all that.

He was very patient; through his patience and work I was able to shoot the rifle and do all the mechanical steps. But when it came to actually shooting the deer, I wasn't able to do that. He never chided me for it; he never made me feel like I wasn't a man. He understood.

He was very thorough and very good at the whole process from teaching us how to handle a weapon, to going out there and using proper safety with it. And because of his patience, he was able to get out there and actually do the hunting without having that immediate deer on the first day. I don't think I had the same level of patience; therefore, I wasn't good at that part. Plus, when it came to actually killing a deer at twelve years of age, it just wasn't something that felt good for me.

The other was that he was always very good at gardening. He would always show me step by step, because that's what his parents did; my grandparents farmed in Mexico for generation after generation and they were all very, very good at it. Dad was exceptional when it came to growing zucchini, corn or any type of vegetable that grows in the Arizona climate of thirty-five hundred to four thousand feet elevation. I still do a lot of gardening on my own. So I know that came from him and his involvement and love of gardening.

*5.* One that really stands out is when he retired from the Cyprus Copper Mine in Bagdad, and there were people who spoke of him and the kind of work he exhibited, his work ethic, and his ability to get the job done.

He worked in a SX plant, which is a solvent extracting plant where they actually sprinkle a watered down, sulphuric acid solution onto the solid copper and extract the copper in a liquid form. Then it gets collected and sent up to an electric plant that converts the liquid copper to solid copper. They would always say he was a lousy farmer because he always sprinkled the solution on the rocks and nothing ever grew; of course it wasn't intended to grow anything, it was supposed to extract copper.

They spoke of how he was working in his late fifties and never complained about the work. The people that came to work for him were entry level workers, and often wouldn't last more than six months because they didn't want to work that hard. His was never to question; his was always to get the job done. And he was a very committed, good person. I think that came out as well; he was a very kind person and that people respected him for both his work ethic and the way he treated others.

And that was very, very rewarding for me. I was very proud of him because he is a man who came to the United States without speaking a word of English. He actually learned English by listening to albums, those big 33s; it would just be nursery rhymes, repeating words. From there, they would get together in small adult learning groups with other workers and copper miners in Bagdad to practice very simple but easy ways to learn English. And he has developed such a great grasp of the English language that he speaks and writes very, very well. He never had any formal education. He only went up to the fifth grade in Mexico, and he left for California at sixteen to work in the strawberry, tomato, and lettuce fields.

He went from that to where he now has a home in Prescott Valley and a home in Mexico; they have very comfortably retired and they split the year between the houses. And all that is from a person that has never had a formal education, but is very intelligent. From his early development to becoming very well established, to his retirement, there are a lot of accomplishments that anybody would be proud of.

6. What I picked up from him was the care and concern in his priority of putting my mom first. For him, it wasn't, "I'm the dominating person in this relationship and I expect you to do this and this." If anything, he went out of his way to ease the burden of six kids being in the house. In our early years, there were actually four of us in a one-bedroom house, and we were all able to live together.

He did as much as he could to ease the pressures of raising kids. He was lifted up from a very mountainous, very small community in Mexico with no electricity or running water. He came to the United States to fit in and to have a family. As they got older, he tried to bring in some of the American culture and way of life, from things as simple as wearing makeup, to my sister wanting to shave her legs. Both were never heard of before on my mom's side when she grew up.

He always protected my mom from all these things. And she was never wrong and he would always tell us that we needed to respect our mom. Period. Even though we knew at times that we were right, to him it didn't matter. Mom was never wrong and we needed to respect her. He really embodies what most people dream of. My wife will say, "Why can't you be more like your dad." (Laughs.) He's set a pretty high level in terms of him being who he is. And it truly is who he is; he's not trying to be somebody he's not. It's just who he is. Even now, I strive to be more like him in those areas. He really had a major impression on me.

7. There are a number of them, but there's one that my kids still even talk about. Every year we would go up to the mountains in the Prescott area in the forest and the pinon trees would have new cones and pinon nuts. Pinon nuts are very flavorful and very good to eat. I would take my two boys and my dad. You don't want to pull the cones down because your hands get full of sap and you collect everything from the pine needles to the dirt. The best way to

get the nuts from the cones is to get up in the tree and shake it. As you shake the branches, the pinon nuts come down to be collected in old bed sheets or plastic we had put on the ground. Then we'd pick out the good ones, and throw the other ones out.

Dad climbed up there in the tree and starting shaking it. All of a sudden, he fell twenty feet. (Laughs.) And my two boys were watching. Dad got up and climbed right back into the tree. Then he started to shake the branches again. So my boys and I were like, "Oh Tata, you're like Superman!" That was about ten years ago; so my youngest was six and my older son was ten. They still talk about, "Remember when Tata fell out of the tree and got back up there and he was still working?"

They now have an image of this Superman husband who really, really (Laughs), treats his wife special. He just keeps growing bigger and bigger as the days go on.


*8.* He actually revealed quite a bit. Just he and I took a trip down to Mexico when I was in my early twenties. We rode the bus down to the state of Guanajuato, and also down to Mexico City. Combined, it was around thirty-four hours on the bus. And it was actually more of getting to know the man than it was anything in particular. We never really had spent any time together as far as a father and son, and in the week that we spent together on that trip, there was just so much that was revealed about him. And I had a better appreciation for him as a father.

When I was younger, impressions were left behind, whether it was the disciplinarian taking the belt to me or spanking me, or how it seemed like I always fell short in meeting his goals. He was such a hard worker; I tended to be not as hard working. I'd do the minimum instead of doing that and then some. I always thought I was never achieving the level of whatever it was that I was asked to do because he did things so well.

On that trip to Mexico, I was able to remove that image of him and enjoy the opportunity to just be with him and develop that father/son relationship. I gained more of an appreciation of the person that he was by being able to just spend quality time with him.

I have since done that myself. My son is in the Marines. And before he went in, we hiked down to the Grand Canyon, stayed at Phantom Ranch, then hiked out again. It was just us spending quality time and connecting. With my younger son, he's not as athletic, so probably hiking the Grand Canyon may not be what we do. But we will do some father/son connection; I think there is value in that.

So I learned to appreciate that experience, and it was more a revealing of the person as opposed to my memories and images of who my father was. It just seemed to break that and create a whole new appreciation for my father. It was a very valuable experience. I think everybody should get the chance to do that with his or her father, grandfather, or mother. It's just a very powerful experience.

*9.* That trip down to Mexico City is the clear memory, just being with him. It was just how savvy he was, like when he wouldn't allow a taxi driver to take advantage of us. As you go into certain parts of the country, there are always forces there that are trying to either get you in a place to take money away from you, or they end up going around thirty miles instead of going directly to a place; what should be a two-minute trip becomes a two-hour trip and you've got to pay too much money.

In every state in Mexico that you cross, there's a manned military presence there of Federales, starting at the border and working all the way down. Dad was able to deal with the people and the situations in very crafty ways. He knew when to slip a ten or a twenty, and when not to. He has always had very, very good people skills and is very intelligent. That trip really revealed a lot to me.

*10.* The traits I would pinpoint are more of patience and hope. There's so much that you invest in your children, and you do the best that you can given the skills that were handed down to you and new skills that you develop. Every child is so unique and so different. You have to be able to understand the uniqueness in each child, and be able to make appropriate adjustments in how you provide the love and the caring that is needed. You also have to understand that there is no one way that's going to work for all of them. Never lose hope, and never communicate that a child is hopeless, or incompetent, or incapable. To break that kind of positive spirit is very detrimental.

My father modeled what he wanted. And even though I never came close to reaching that expectation, he never made me feel like I was inferior. Although at times, he would make some comments more in jest than anything else about how, "Here you are so young and so strong, and you're allowing your old man to outdo you." I don't know if that was for the purpose of trying to motivate me to prove him wrong or what. But it was never done in a malicious manner.

Just have patience and always maintain hope for your child and help him or her feel capable. Never make them feel like they are inferior or incompetent.

# CHAPTER 47

# Michael

*1.* Michael Flannigan, and I'm thirty-one years of age.

*2.* I call (Laughs), that's funny, I refer to my biological father as Old Mike. When I call him on the phone to talk to him, I refer to him as Old Man. I usually go, "Hey, what's up Old Man?" And when I'm in the presence of family members like his mother, my biological grandmother, I call him Dad of course. But when I'm having a conversation with other people, I refer my original dad as Tim. It's kind of hard to explain because I do have three fathers and I have called them all Dad at different points in time. I refer to my biological father mostly as Tim and my dad in parentheses.

The man that raised me primarily, Gary, whom I've recently got back into contact with after many years, I call him Dad a lot. I call him Dad the most because he was there when I was two until my parents got divorced when I was twelve and was in junior high. We had visitation until I was fifteen, and then he and I had a falling out because of some crap. And it was kind of a rough divorce, especially with me being the stepson. I never realized how much he really loved me until I got reacquainted with him recently. But he's the one I refer to as my dad; he was there through the growing years.

By the time I was sixteen, my mom got remarried and I was pretty much a man. I was already six feet tall and two hundred pounds. He, I call Joe; I never call him Dad, simply because by the time he came around, I was the man of the house. So that's how the dad thing goes.

3. Which father? It's funny; my dad that raised me is gentler than I remember him as a child. He's always worked hard. He owned his own small town business; he had a good sense of business. He was the garbage man in town with his brother. My grandfather retired from the business; he owned the school buses in our small town and the trash removal company. When Grandfather retired, my dad and his brother split the company so my dad got all the residential business and his brother got all the commercial business.

But he's always been a very hard worker—busted his back to put food on the table. And he's a pretty well respected guy in the community. He was on the city council and things like that. He was pretty social; everybody knows the name of the family because they owned two of the larger businesses in town. He was well known and well liked in the community

Yeah. Now that I can look at him man to man, as opposed to looking up to him as dad, I can definitely see those qualities about him.


4. (Laughs.) Golf. Golf was his passion, aside from his work. Every guy has got to have his escape; golf was Dad's escape and his thing. (Laughs.) It's funny; I was just thinking about this the other day. He taught me how to play golf and also how to maintain the clubs.

I remember him taking me in and showing me how to scrub up the clubs and how to dig out all the green divot crap in the grooves on the irons. He told me, "Maintain the golf clubs and take pride in your clubs, because you're only as good as your clubs." (Laughs.) We had a grungy bathroom in the basement and I remember him in that bathroom teaching me how to maintain the golf clubs.


5. Golf was his game but he also played softball. I remember him being in the softball league and seeing him crack a few out of the park. That made me proud. I was kind of like the little mascot of the team—they used to call us all Burgie. I've picked up other nicknames since, but they used to call me Little Burgie and I had

a little baseball jersey just like the team wore. I used to run around the park and people would say, "Hey, there's Little Burgie."

I remember a few times when he cracked one out and I was like, "Yeah. That's the Old Man. That's Dad."

6. His sensitivity. When the divorce was going on, it was pretty emotional. I remember seeing him cry for the first time and I realized the softer side of him.

And then again when we got reacquainted, I realized how much sensitivity he had; we had a couple of crying moments. He came to town recently; I've been here eleven years and I haven't seen him in eleven years. And before that, between the ages of sixteen and twenty, I didn't really see him at all. So it had been fifteen years of no contact. No, "Hey, how are you doing?" No phone calls. No nothing. My brothers are all his sons; I was the stepson. My half brothers are very close to him. Over time my brothers have said, "Dad really wants to see you. You really should call him." And finally I got up the gumption to call him.

When I called him, he got quivery with me on the phone and he came out. A guy goes through a lot of changes from fifteen to thirty-one years of age, you know. I'm fricking losing my hair, and I'm much more mature. From what he remembers, I was a chunky fifteen-year-old kid. We both said, "Oh my God. Where have we been all these years?" And we had this moment. We both were feeling each other and said, "I've missed you." I didn't realize how much I missed the guy.

And he said, " I wanted to be there for you. I remember wanting to help you in those years. I didn't help you with college," like he had my brothers. And anytime they got in trouble, or needed help financially, he was always there for them.

I really didn't realize the sensitivity he had in him and how much I really picked up the sensitive side from him. We have stayed close since. He had to bail me out of jail a couple of weeks ago. It's not like, "Oh man, here's an opportunity that I can get some money out of him after all these years." I hadn't relied on him, even though before we had been close. I call him more than I do Tim, my biological dad, or my mom's husband Joe, who's a wonderful guy. It's funny about Joe; he's ten years older than me and ten years younger than my mom, and I was already a man when I met him. But he's a very nice guy and he's very good for my mom.

But I've been communicating a lot more with my dad, Gary, ever since he came down and visited a few months ago; I feel like there's a big gap that needed to be filled in and a lot of time that needed to be made up. I'm looking forward to seeing him again. He works for a company now that does well drilling, so he's out of state a lot. And they say they'll fly him back anywhere he calls home. So he's going to use one of those coming home times to stay for a week and we're going to go see ball games and stuff like that.

It really surprised me to see how eager he was to help get me out of jail. We all have those moments where we screw up and end up going to jail. And I hated to ask him. He thought I was joking because I was supposed to be going up to Minnesota to vacation and I ended up going to jail the night before I was to leave. I called him collect because I was like, "Crap. I don't want to sit in jail for a month. Crap. What am I going to do?" I'm pretty sure I could have gotten a loan out of my bosses, but I'd hate to do that.

So I called him and he was more than eager; he was running around transferring funds from his account to my sister's account, just going out of his way. And there were times when we couldn't communicate because I was in jail and you can only make collect calls and they don't have the best quality phones in jail. There were times when he was calling my fiancé, and she conveyed to me how emotional he was getting. The sensitivity of him was coming out and he was scared for me; he was feeling my pain. He and I were very much in tune. It's crazy; I didn't realize how in tune we were because we were gone from each other for so long. The father/son being in tune thing is what I feel from him, more than my biological father or my mother's current husband. It's weird what a connection we have.

7. I used to help him out in the summertime. He had the trash removal business in town. And in the summertime I used to love

to go with him. When I was nine through eleven, I used to ride along with him and help him. I'd sit passenger side and jump off the truck. Sometimes I'd ride on the back of the truck like you've seen in the movies; sometimes I would be that guy.

I felt like a little man. I'd get into my old grungy work clothes, get on the truck, and race him to the cans. It felt cool to pull the lever and make the whole (Laughs) trash compacter go. That was a fine memory of helping him out in the summer. I didn't really expect any money from him but he'd throw me a few bucks and buy me something at Dairy Queen. It was just more of the bonding thing.

You can find some good stuff in that trash. It's surprising what people throw away, especially people that are pretty well off. Like they say, "One man's trash is another man's treasure." And it's true, you can find good stuff. It's not like I'm a dumpster diver or anything, but you'd be surprised with what you come across.

*8.* The connection that we have. There were so many years that were lost. There's just a connection.

*9.* I would have to say that would be a more recent one. When he came a few months ago, he could only visit for a couple days, but it was a couple of good, quality days. We talked a lot and ironed out some stuff because he didn't know how I perceived him. I'm my mom's oldest son, so obviously I'm my mom's boy. You know?

He thought that I hated him. There were bad times, but I never hated the guy. He was worried that my mom had twisted up my perception of him. Which was probably partially correct, but he was really worried. We reconnected on a loving level, and we had a real long conversation at a restaurant. We sat and had a couple of beers and had dinner. My fiancé was there with her little boy, who is growing up in such a similar circumstance to mine that it is uncanny how much he and I have in common; but that's a totally different story.

But we had a good, long, heart to heart that really meant a hell of a lot to him and it meant a lot to me, too, because I didn't want him to think that. And he was really worried that I was having hateful feelings or hated him all these years. We just lost contact. And I went on with my life, followed a path that I chose, and for a while never looked back. And then it just felt good to reconnect. It really did.

*10.* The balance of firmness and love—it's got to be there. You have to be the strong hand of the household but you got to remember that for every strong moment, you've got to have that moment of praise or take your son aside and show him how much you love him or go to the park with him. It's got to be the balance.

# CHAPTER 48

# Mathew

*1.* My interview name is Mathew, and my real age is fifty-three.

*2.* I call my father two different things—Dad and Poopsie. Poopsie was a name that my brother, who is a year and a half older than I, came up with and it's just the two of us that use that name with my dad.

*3.* People from the outside would describe him professionally, and would describe him as extremely competent, extremely professional, extremely thorough, a community leader—a great guy, a great sense of humor. That was his persona on the outside; that's how other people perceived him. Not family members, or other people.

I really can't say much about his professional life because that was kind of kept separate from the family. I mean, he was very successful, as he spent most of his life there. So I'm assuming that's an indicator of success.

But I did not know his professional life very much other than I saw his activities in the various community organizations like Kiwanis and those kinds of things. And people always spoke very, very highly of him. He appeared in the newspaper and all those kinds of things. My impression of him was that he was very successful and that I would agree with that persona based on that perception.

*4.* Boy, that's a tough one. I can vividly remember him giving me my first baseball mitt and then playing catch with me; I can't remember exactly how old I was. That, and as a family we would frequently go to Jackson Hole, Wyoming and fish the Snake River.

It was a big deal with my dad. In fact, it was kind of a coming of age when we got to go with Dad—just the boys and Dad to Jackson Hole. But we would also go as a family. And he taught me how to fish the river. And I'm really trying to focus on those that I really perceive as very positive experiences. Learning to play catch and then learning to fish the Snake River. I will come back to the Snake River.

*5.* I was living in Seal Beach, California, and I would have been twenty-five. The International Kiwanis Convention was being held in San Diego. I drove the two hours down to San Diego and my dad was announced as the International Vice-president of Kiwanis at this convention with thousands and thousands of Kiwanians from all over the world. Experiencing that made me very, very proud. He would have been sixty-four at the time because he was thirty-nine when I was born.

And I got to see my mother and him be the celebrities at the convention social events because they invited me to come; I was the only family member that was there. I was very proud of him. All of my moments of pride are tempered with other feelings, but... (Laughs).

*6.* Either fortunately or unfortunately, depending on what seat you're sitting in, I have a number of his behaviors and attitudes. Probably the strongest one is that I'm very much like him when it comes to money. That is very unfortunate because I'm not able to really enjoy the fruits of my labor as much as I would like to because I'm constantly worrying about money.

Growing up, he was always very adamant about not being excessive, buying only what you need. He had a you-can-make-that-last kind of mentality. Even on vacation you couldn't splurge; you couldn't just do something whimsically or just for the heck of it and spend money. You had to be very controlled, just very tight (Laughs), with your money. I have definitely picked up that behavior. My wife and children continue to work on me (Laughs), but not with a great deal of success.

7. Probably my favorite stories, my fondest memories are from fishing in Jackson Hole. Fishing and golfing. We would often times fish in the morning and then go out and play golf at the Jackson Hole Country Club in the afternoon. For several years, because I was the youngest and we went every summer, it would be only my dad and I because everybody else was away at college and/or working; those were probably my fondest memories with him.

Once again, all of the emotional aspects of our relationship were taken out of that picture because we were sharing a common love for fishing and golfing. And we were on an equal playing field relative to the whole experience. Those are probably my fondest memories, the ones I cherish the most.

But also, the big deal was taking my brothers; we would all go together. And then as I got older, of course we'd go out to the bars at night and that kind of thing. He became a different person when he was up there. He loved Jackson Hole and went up there several times every year, not just when he went with us. Up there he was a different man; he was just more playful and that type of thing. So those are probably my fondest memories.

8. Two things—I really can't narrow it to just one. As I learned more and more about his management of finances, that one really surprised me. Given what I've previously said about his tightness and concern with money, I was surprised at just how poorly he managed and invested money and how he really never built his medical practice into the success he could have.

It was very surprising to see, even as recently as fifteen years ago. He's now ninety-two. He practiced medicine until he was eighty-three, and he was still charging people five dollars for an office visit. He was proud of being the cheapest doctor in town, but that lack of both personal and business management of finances really impacted the family over time. And I was totally unaware of that until I got older. Other than the fact that I knew he was very tight with money, we always had a nice house and so on, but I just assumed that he was financially successful and secure and managed his money.

Had my mother not been in an investment club and invested over the last forty years, we would be in a much different financial situation with them then we are. They are able to pay for their own apartment and that type of thing. But without my mother's investing, that would have never happened. He simply did not invest; he mismanaged the money in terms of investment, and that was very surprising to me. My knowledge of it began twenty years ago, and has evolved to where I now have full disclosure of what he did money wise.

Probably something that I did realize in the last ten years that kind of surprised me was connecting his behaviors as I was growing up to how selfish he is. And watching, even now with his relationship with my mother, how everything is about him. Even when she recently almost died, he was totally unaware of that even though part of that now is his current mental state. But it's just been interesting. And that surprises me. But that helps me a little bit because I can now connect that selfishness with some of the many things that he did as I was growing up that I really never understood.

Those two things—probably the most was the money thing. That to me was just very, very surprising, that a very successful man, both in his profession and in the community, simply did not attend to the financial matters that could have and would have helped his family.

I think back about the fact that the only money I got from my parents to go to college was the money my mom snuck me. And I think back, my dad was a doctor, and the only money I got was the hundred dollar bills my mom would sneak me when I came home on weekends.

*9.* Well once again, I have two. This is a great example of my dad's very, very, strict upbringing, and his extreme tightness with finances. I can remember being a young boy, and my dad was shaving while I was sitting on the toilet going to the bathroom. And I went to get the toilet paper to wipe, and I pulled out some toilet paper.

And he looked down at me and said, "You don't need that much. You only need six sheets." I vividly remember that. I can picture the bathroom, and that was in our house that would have been three houses ago! I can see myself sitting on the toilet in total disbelief. But, I used the six sheets. And went on.

The other times I picture my father again go back to Jackson Hole. I vividly remember several instances of catching good fish and him being there. And playing golf. Again, those are probably the fondest memories that I have of him and me together.

Those two memories are at opposite ends of the spectrum (Laughs), in terms of positive and negative. It was pretty interesting, both of those experiences.

*10.* I'm going to say two things. To be the best father you can be—the most important things are selflessness and the ability to unconditionally give and receive love. For a father or a mother to be an influence in their kid's life, they have to be able to step out of themselves and give and receive unconditional love. Giving love with conditions creates problems; it can influence kids in a negative way if they constantly think that they have to earn love or aren't able to give love to their father. Therein lies some of the difficulties that evolved in my experiences as a son, because my father was never able to do either one of those two things.

Being selfless and loving unconditionally are the biggest challenges as a parent. It requires the ability to not care for yourself first, but to care for your children first and to still love them no matter what they do, even if you don't like their behaviors or their decisions. Those are the two most important things that a father can do.

Never under-estimate how important a father is.

# CHAPTER 49

# Andrew

*1.* Andrew, sixty-four.

*2.* I call my father Dad, and I think it was just traditional. Everybody else did that. Those ahead of me called him Dad and I fell into that. Dad.

*3.* Let me set the stage here. When I was born, my mother was not married and she was seventeen years old. So she gave me to my grandparents. My grandfather, who I called Dad, raised me from a baby and he's the only dad that I knew. I did not meet my biological father until I was sixteen. So for the sake of clarification, my dad is not my biological dad, but he's the person who raised me.

They would describe him as a very, very religious man, not an extremist, but one who internalized religious principles into what he did every day in terms of honorableness and integrity. He was a hard worker, extremely hard working. He was incredibly faithful, and very dependable. He was an interesting type of disciplinarian in that he believed very much in right and wrong, but he was very compassionate. He was not so insistent that you did things his way, but that you chose the path that you understood to be the right path.

Loving, certainly supportive. He could be aloof from time to time because he had his crosses to bear in terms of dilemmas and issues that he dealt with. So when he was going through his thing, from time to time he withdrew somewhat from the normal conversation expected out of him. Playful. He had a great sense of humor; he was a funny guy.

Very dependable. You knew what to expect. He was steady as a rock. If I were picking a characteristic that I remember more than anything else, it would be his devotion to what he felt was Truth. He thought that it was very important for a guy to be very truthful and honorable in what he did.

I do. I do. I've found in my lifetime that it's been hard to live up to some of those expectations, but I still see them as things that I'd like to achieve at some point. They are a nice bedrock for building your relationships in life.

*4.* In addition to being a minister, he was a carpenter. He used to build houses; he was very good at it. He taught me some carpentry skills, but in a very slow, somewhat guiding fashion. I pulled nails from wood for hours before I actually got a chance to do something else. He would teach that nothing was acceptable unless it was right on. It had to be level; it had to be straight, and if not, then you needed to redo it. So from a physical perspective, he taught me some carpentry skills. I wish I had paid more attention and put more of it into application, because I could have saved a lot of money.

But there was a life skill he taught me that was even more lasting to me. I define it as perpetual hope, that you have this optimism that things can work out if you allow them to and if you stay with it. From a life perspective, he didn't give up. And that's proven to be invaluable with me because there are many relationships that I would have given up on; I would have washed them out had I not had that as a reference point. And there were times when he could have and should have given up on stuff that I was doing, but he didn't. I can look back and think that maybe it's worth hanging in there.

So there were two skills. One was carpentry. I still appreciate it, and still dabble in it, not that I'm particularly proficient in it. But I still enjoy it, and it is reminiscent of the times I spent with him.

But the life skill, that stick-to-it-tive-ness has proven very, very worthwhile to me.

Let me just go back to that one lesson he taught me. When I was a kid growing up, I enjoyed syrup and biscuit. It's not particularly nourishing or nutritious and has very little food value. But I enjoyed it. The problem was that I would have syrup and biscuit and it would mess up my appetite so I wouldn't be hungry.

One of the many jobs my dad had was that he drove the school bus and I used to ride that school bus. After school, he would drop me off at home on the way to finishing the last twelve miles of his route.

And he would continually remind me, "Don't get in the syrup and biscuit because it will mess up your appetite. So, stay out of it."

He dropped me off one day and I had this unquenchable urge for syrup and biscuit and just sort of fell victim to it. He came back over an hour later and we started talking. About the third or fourth sentence out of his mouth was, "How many times have I told you not to have syrup and biscuit." And I was thinking, "This guy was driving a bus and he was gone, and how in the world could he have known that?"

So I lied. I just flat lied. I said, "Aw Dad, I didn't have that."

And he said, "You know lying is really bad," and gave me a nice little sermon; but I stuck to my guns and got my normal restriction and punishment.

Years later, I was a sophomore in college; we were sitting on the porch one day and I said, "Do you remember when I got in trouble with that syrup and biscuit?"

And it took him a few minutes for him to recall it and he said, "Oh, yes." I never lied to him since. I figured he had a connection with the guy upstairs, and he could see through these lies and stuff so the lesson I learned was—don't ever lie to him.

So I asked him, "How in the world did you know that I had syrup and biscuit when you were gone?"

He said, "Oh, yes. I walked in the door and I looked at your shoes, and it was on your shoes. A drop of syrup was on your shoes."

That experience caused me to never lie to him again. And I think back; had I not had that experience, I probably would have tried lying to him about other things and they would have backfired. I'm sure they wouldn't have worked out well. It's a funny story. I started to write a book about my life; that story was in it and my oldest daughter thought that was a pretty funny story, too.

5. There are several that I react to without thinking about it. He had a lot of land, a lot of land for where we lived, and it was under continuous siege at one point. And I can remember a couple of instances when people were actively trying to take the land, and the manipulative and hateful stuff they had undertaken. I remember a conversation that he had with two of the guys that were involved, and they were verbally assassinating him—what we would certainly call verbal abuse now. They came at him over and over and over again. He stood his ground and he maintained his composure. He was very insistent and defiant. He said, "No, I'm not going to do that. No, you're not going to get that land." I was a little kid; I was in the fifth grade so I was ten years old.

I've often thought about what courage that took. It would have been easier for him to fly off the handle or to cave in and he chose to do neither; he just stood his ground.

6. I think that my association with Rev, my dad, gave me a level of courage that I don't think I would have normally developed because of his concept of seeing it through, and not bailing out or giving in. I watched him model that day in and day out, and my courage comes directly from my living with him until I was seventeen, when I went away to school. There are many other things, but that one sticks out in my mind.

7. My favorite story is the one about the syrup and biscuit. We had a lot of good times. When I got my license, I became kind of like his driver, his chauffeur. He had churches that were out of town and we spent a lot of time riding, going back and forth. I spent three, four, days a week involved with some sort of church

activity and there were a lot of stories and things that happened in and around the church. But my favorite story, without a doubt, is the syrup on the shoe. I remember that one so vividly.

I also remember this instance. They raised a lot of other children, including my mother, but I was the last one. I was a junior in high school and I was running track. We were working on a house, and we were getting ready to finish up and go. It had been a long day. My job was tearing down stuff, not building. We were walking back to the front road; we had almost a quarter mile to go. And he said, "You think you're pretty fast, don't you?"

"Well yeah," I said. I was fast.

"I challenge you to a race," he said.

"Okay," I said. So we took off running. He stayed with me until we got almost to the end, and then he pushed a little ahead.

I was all in and he said. "Well you see, a grown man can still run, too." That was a part of that humanness, that closeness that we had.

He was very articulate as is the case with most itinerant ministers. They develop a vocabulary to reflect in communication, and he used that to interact a lot with people. I think that because I was the last, none came after me, I was treated like the baby in the family. I don't think that I was spoiled, but as I look at the other kids that they raised ahead of me, I do think I received a little special treatment on the way, which was good.

8. I was surprised that he had an affair. Blew me away. I started writing a book in '91. My oldest daughter was visiting once and she said, "You know Dad, you've done a lot of interesting stuff over your life and you need to write that stuff down because we don't all know it and it'd be kind of nice to share it." At the time she was home schooling her children.

So I said, "Well, that sounds interesting." And with that, I started doing some research. I think every family has that relative that just knows everything about the family tree. In mine, it was Aunt Jack. She had sent me some research stuff and I had gone through it so I couldn't wait to get back and talk to her.

I went home to Alabama after I had written her and told her what I was doing, and she said, "Are you sure you want to do this?"

I said, " Yeah, I really do." I was getting excited about it.

And she said, "Well, you know, there's some places I found where the tree doesn't divide quite right." I thought that was quite funny and then she went on to tell me about some of our family, and some of it was pretty shocking.

This affair just blew my mind because I knew the lady. She was in the church. She was one of the people in the choir, and an assistant choir director. And the reason we found out about it was because they had a child. And I ended up knowing the child. And I didn't find out about any of this until after he had passed away. Very interesting, very interesting. I was shocked.

9. We spent a lot of time together in the car. I can remember several trips during which I would ask him to tell me about his dad, or tell me what he did when he was a kid. Some how or another we don't quite see our parents as kids. I'm sure that in the back of our minds we know they had to be at some point, and we wonder what they enjoyed doing or whatever.

I remember one ride from Lenin back to Tuscaloosa when he was talking about his childhood. He told me about his five other brothers and the stuff that they did when they were growing up. He talked about how distant his father was. His father worked a lot and really didn't have time to spend with them; I'm sure it was a function of time rather than desire. I remember that conversation because I could see and hear a sense of disappointment in him, and I realized that Dad wished that he had had a different kind of relationship with his father. I think that may have been one of the reasons that Dad raised the number of children that he did and tried to maintain his closeness to them. So off the top of my head, that one stands alone.

10. I think you've got to be honest and model that for your children while interacting in a consistent fashion. I would say hon-

esty in just being who you are, with all your shortcomings, and not being afraid to acknowledge that they exist. And even talk about them with your children and your family if it's necessary.

Be honest to the point of being accessible. Don't hide behind work or other stuff. You need to be there so that they can see that you are a mortal. When you screw up, you need to own it, because if you don't, it's hard for them to.

Be honest. As a father, you owe them honesty.

# CHAPTER 50

# Bob

*1.* Bob. And my age is forty-one.

*2.* Anymore I call him Pop. Actually I picked it up from a friend of mine; it hit me as something very personal and endearing, versus everybody calling his or her parent Dad or Daddy; I guess a few stuffed shirts use Father. I just thought Pop was a very casual, yet respectful and an endearing way to approach him or greet him or address him.

*3.* He's just an awesome guy. Everybody stops by his house to see him. He's good-natured and willing to do anything at any time. He loves to piddle around and do stuff and he wants to get up and go. Everybody I know tells me about what an incredible father I have. Still to this day, all my siblings and I have friends that will go by to see him just to say hello; we're near the holiday season and sure enough, his doorbell will ring quite often with people from several generations. He's very approachable. There would have to be a good reason for him to ever look down on somebody. He's just a great guy.

Oh yeah. I'm very blessed.

*4.* Dad's a college graduate and a retired school administrator; he was basically a white-collar worker his whole life. His father was a machinist and Dad picked up working with tools and stuff like that as a hobby. So the general skill that he taught me and passed on to me is that of craftsmanship. He gave me the skills to build a wall, run some wire, or hang a fan. He taught me how to do it and do it right. One of his big things that he taught me, especially in the crafts end of it, would be finish the job. Make sure you finish the job. He used to always tell us the story about his brother, my uncle, and how he once hung paneling and finished it with ten-penny, flat head nails.

And when you finish a job, make sure you finish it properly and make it look nice. He's willing to take his time, not get in a rush, and do it right. Do it right the first time so you don't have to bother with it again, and finish it so it looks as nice as it can.

5. There's been several there too. I would have to say his retirement party. Being an administrator is kind of like being a president. People either love you or they hate you. Obviously a lot times people show to a party out of mere obligation, but that was not the sense or feeling at all. It was really a huge celebration and they were sorry to see him go. It wasn't just one person sitting there telling me my dad did a really good job. He was genuinely loved and respected. I really got that sense all at one time from a huge group of people, almost to an overwhelming standpoint. That culminated his whole career. At that point in time it was, "Okay, he's the man."

6. Compassion. I'd say compassion. That's probably why he's Dad. That's why everybody likes him. Growing up, he was a disciplinarian. Toe the line, this, that, whatever; but Dad is an extremely compassionate man. You would probably not know it at first meeting because there's a lot under the shell with Dad. Yeah, compassion by a long shot.

7. There have been so many through camping to just sitting around talking. I love this one because it really was just that way. I don't know if you've been a fan of it or watched it, but Dad was very Andy-Griffith-like. In the *Andy Griffith Show*, Andy always had the right advice and he always put it in a way you really couldn't

argue with. It is kind of ironic because we are sitting in a high school classroom.

It was my senior year, second semester. One afternoon Dad came home and we were just sitting there chatting. And he asked me a question that hit me like a ton of bricks. He said, "So, what do you plan on doing when you graduate?" And all of a sudden there was this extreme immediacy. It was like, "Wow, the ride's over. And I have to do something here, don't I?" He let me sit there and hem and haw a little and then I said, "I guess I'm gonna get a job."

And he replied, "May I suggest that you at least take a couple classes at the community college." Obviously being a school administrator, he was pro-education all the way. And then he said, "If you're not sure what you want to do, take a couple classes that you can use no matter what you do, like English and math, and you get them out of the way. Then if you wake up in a year or two and what you decide on involves school, great; you've already got a lot of the basics out of the way. And if it doesn't involve school, it doesn't hurt you one bit, and you certainly haven't hurt yourself by improving your education."

That just made way too much sense. As much as any high school senior, I wasn't a huge advocate of school; I didn't want to be a life-long student. I had been looking for a good excuse, or a good reason, or a good way not to go to school; but Jesus, that made sense. And it basically happened just like that. I went to the community college and I took nine or twelve hours each semester and I eventually ended up getting a degree.

But yeah, there were a lot of favorite times, fun times. But that was just the type of thing, a dawning that really lumps in with his compassion. Dad used to guide by a gentle, gentle hand. And that just made way too much sense.

8. I was surprised at how much he was like me. Or how much I'm like him and the fact that he was just so rambunctious as a youngster. And how wild he was when he was younger and all the wild and stupid stuff that they did. You never think your dad was capable of that.

And probably even more so than any of my brothers, it's surprising how just uncanny alike Dad and I are. It's kind of like a
husband and wife that have been together for sixty years and are
almost twins. One of us can just be thinking something and the
other will be thinking it as well. We're actually quite in tune that
way. When I was younger, I was rambunctious and did some stupid
things myself which follows the pattern; we are so much alike in
that way. So yeah, just that fact that he was young and stupid and
crazy like I was.

9. Dad and I have always been close. When I was eighteen
and in my first year of college, he had a weeklong superintendent's
convention in New Orleans. A lot of times when Dad had conven-
tions, he would pay for Mom to fly with him and she would piddle
around while he went to his meetings and then they would turn the
rest into vacations. I guess they'd already been to New Orleans.

So, I was sleeping in one morning and Mom came in and
would dust one item and leave, and then five minutes later come
in and adjust the blinds and leave. She did this about fifteen times
and I finally said, "What is it, Mom? What do you need, what do
you want?"

And she leaned over and asked me, "I was just wondering, if
you could take the time off from school, would you like to go to
New Orleans, stay with your dad, and spend some time in New
Orleans?"

"Oh boy, would I!" That night I caught a red eye flight and
hopped a shuttle from the airport to the hotel and met up with
Dad. And he and I spent a week in New Orleans. Every morning
he'd go to his meetings and then we'd meet at noon at the Super-
dome's clubhouse. Then we took off to see Bourbon Street and the
French Quarter and a bunch of different sites. We just had a blast
for six straight days. It was just him and me. It was kind of cool.

10. Forgiveness. It would be forgiveness. Because no matter
how perfect kids are, eventually everybody does something wrong
sometime. You just can't hold on to it. I'm sure my dad made mis-

takes and his dad let it go. And I did and Dad had to let it go. And I'm sure one day my girl's going do something and I'm going have to let it go. Sometimes you've just got to bite your tongue and show compassion and forgiveness.

# CHAPTER 51

# Diego

*1.* I'm Diego. Fifty-six years and eleven months.

*2.* My brothers and I all call him Daddy. And we always have, even as adults. Just probably because that's what my older brother used when I learned to talk. Never changed. Never was Dad, Poppa or Father. Daddy always.

*3.* Reticent—a man of few words. Very likable, but he does not like other people. He's a bit of a misanthrope, becoming more and more so. But other people like him, very helpful. He's got that old-fashioned, Depression era, strong, silent type, Gary Cooper thing.

Yes, it's the only side of him I've ever seen.

*4.* This is about him not teaching me a skill—the famous fifteen and a half year old boy with the standard transmission. He was in the passenger seat, I let out the clutch, the truck lurched about six times, and died.

He said, "Stop being silly," and got out of the truck and went in the house.

He told my older brother, "Go out there and teach him how to drive." So my eighteen-and-a-half year old brother came out and taught me how to drive a stick shift.

I remember him teaching me how to tie my shoes, but other than that, he never had the patience to follow through on a teaching job.

*5.* I was delivering the *Denver Post*; I had eighty papers on my route. It was a Sunday morning, and the papers weighed about a thousand pounds each. And there had been a blizzard. I got up and I went out, and I was brushing the snow off my bicycle.

And my dad, who was a working man on a Sunday morning at five, got up and said, "You sit on the tailgate of the truck." It was the same one, by the way, with the stick shift. "And I'll drive through this snowstorm and you toss your papers from the back of the truck." He didn't have to do that. I don't know if I was proud, but I sure was happy.

*6.* Oh heavens, everything. I am my father's son. I am impatient. I am misanthropic, sometimes. I am anal-retentive.

There are two ways you can react to a father; one is to leave the battlefield, and the other is to become him. I've tried to become him with pretty much everything. Behaving like him has cost me two marriages.

*7.* It's a story about my dad, but not during my lifetime. He was a high school dropout that had such incredible reflexes and vision that he became a pilot during World War II. And through a series of bizarre events, he finished first in his class in flight school. Not because he was the best, but because he got sick, got recycled into the next class, and came in right as they were about to take a test he'd already taken. He got the highest score and finished first in his class. That caused them to then make him an instructor rather than send him to combat.

Based on that, I'm here. It's quite possible I would not be here had he gone the other direction, had he not gotten sick, not gotten recycled, and then made a flight instructor. That's my kind of war hero.

*8.* (Immediately.) That he wasn't big. I thought he was the biggest, strongest man on earth. He's five eight, a hundred and forty pounds. That's not a big man. He wears a size six and a half shoe. I thought he had arms like Popeye and that he could lift a house.

Now I realize he was a little, tiny guy. Who knew?

*9.* When my mother was sick, he was a different person. When he was Dad in the house, he was a traditional fifties dad—stern, aloof, came home from work, read the paper. When my mom was sick, he was the parent; he took both roles. He made it better; it was more fun to be with him. Not that I wanted my mother to be sick, but she was always kind of frail. It was kind of cool, kind of a cool house, kind of like a *My Three Sons* type of environment, just the dad and the boys. It was all right.

*10.* Patience. Patience. There are lots of things I can't do now because my dad didn't teach me because he wasn't patient enough to finish the job. I inherited and mimicked his impatience so I didn't teach myself either. I know there are skills that other guys have learned from their fathers, and I never have.

So I think any father has to be patient. You can't ever assume that one try is ever going get something done; it's not going to happen. Patience.

# CHAPTER 52

# Tommy

*1.* My name is Tommy, and I'm twenty-five.

*2.* I call him Father because he was in and out of my life very frequently. And there are certain situations when he wasn't there on days that I consider special days.

On my eighth birthday, I wanted nothing more but to see him. He wasn't wealthy, so he rode the bus to get around and he said he'd be at my house to pick me up so we could go to the school to play. From what my mom tells me, I got dressed about an hour early. I specifically remember looking out the door every five minutes to see if his bus had passed by. He never got off. I called him the next day, because he never called me. And he said that he had other important things to do.

My dad was in my life up until the age of eight. And then he was in and out of my life until fifteen. And then he got deported back to Mexico because of drug issues. Even though he's been here since he was three, he never got his citizenship. So he had a green card the whole time. He recently got stripped of that green card and now he's trying to get it pardoned by the President. Right now, we just have frequent phone call conversations back and forth.

*3.* It depends who you ask. People always say my dad had good intentions, they just never came out correctly. He was very easy to manipulate by the crowds that he would hang around with. They would always bring him back to the drugs side whenever he got out of jail. There was a certain neighborhood; if he crossed the street, we all knew that he was going to start; that's what we called it.

My mom's side of the family would say he's a good man. He just didn't have the moral support. His mom, I guess you would call her a kook, she was crazy; she was off the wall. His father separated from his mom at an early age, and his mom went to go remarry someone else and left him in Arizona at the age of sixteen to be raised by his older brother and sister. So that side of the family tends to say that he is the best, and I think they say that because they feel guilty for not raising him properly because he's the youngest of seven children.

From what I remember, most of all he's a hard working man. He was a good interviewer; I remember him getting really good jobs at UPS and FedEx. The times that he was in my life, he got me anything I wanted. When we were together as a family, we had a pretty good life. He's a very hard working man and I think a lot of people would say that he is now.

He's a warrior of the streets too, because he knows how to survive on the streets. You could give him a dollar-fifty and he could make it last for three days; he knows how to find shelter.

4. I was probably about six years old; he was teaching me how to ride a bike. It was my first day riding and I wanted to ride with the training wheels. We bought it with training wheels and he let me ride it for ten minutes and he came back outside and said, "You're going to learn to ride it right like everyone else." And I didn't want to. I remember crying a lot. And he took off the training wheels. We practiced until six that night.

That's probably when I first remember him not being mean, but being very stern in his ways. I think he wanted me to succeed, or be something that he wasn't. So his anger came out a lot in little events like that, where if I didn't do it right, we had to sit there for hours on end to make sure I did it right.

I remember falling a lot. He'd say, "Get back up." My knees and my jeans were torn. My mom came out of the apartment and yelled for him to leave me alone. And he wouldn't stop. I remember him saying back, "He's my son, too." But I was an only child, no brother or sister to switch with and have my father pick on them for a little while.

5. I have two instances that really stand out in my mind. I was about eight years old and we lived in a raunchy apartment and I told him I wanted a telescope. And I begged and begged for this telescope. And I woke up on Christmas Day and there was a telescope out there. I remember that Christmas night we stayed out on the patio trying to find the moon in the dark. I remember looking at him and I was awed by the fact that I thought he knew astronomy and what the moon was made of, and how all that worked.

I can't confirm the other time. I graduated high school early, as a junior, and my dad's side of the family says that he was there. They said that he was in the back behind the bushes because he didn't want to be embarrassed by my mom's side of the family. He even tells me he was there.

I guess I hold on to that because it's one of my last memories of when he was in America to see my world before he got deported back. I really wanted him to be there so I could feel his presence. He says he watched me walk on the podium to get my diploma.

6. My aunt used to be on the staff of the *Wallace and Ladmo Show* in Arizona. I used to watch them every morning before I went to school. And she got me on the show. I remember him taking me there and actually he was the one who negotiated with my aunt to get me on the show. I was exited. The good memories I carry with me are the minimal bonding times that we had.

I also remember him being on the roof when I went to my Grandma's house. So I asked my Grandma, "Where is he?"

"He's on the roof," she said.

So I went on the roof and he was sitting with his legs dangling off the edge. He said, "Come over here and sit by me."

I said, "No. I'm fine." I wanted to stay in the middle of the roof.

And he said, "No. Come here." He was being that dad of when

I was six, riding the bike. So I went over there because I knew he wouldn't stop until I did.

And he told me things like women would pay to have sex with him and he would do it. And how he would still do drugs, and where he would always go when he was with his friends. He tried to give me advice, and I knew he had good intentions. One of his advices was, "If you're going to steal, don't steal something small and petty. If you're going to steal, steal big, so you know it was worth it." I could never interpret that as good advice, but I know somewhere in there he had good intentions.

Actually there was one physical thing. His dad had given him a pair of little plastic dolls that looked like Wallace and Ladmo, but they were the originals. One had a Charlie Chaplin moustache and the other was his sidekick; I don't know what the characters were. He said, "These are very rare." I remember the bottom shoe of the fat guy was chipping and on the other guy, the hat was chipping. And the clothes were very torn. They looked very abused, but to him they were in mint condition. He wanted me to have them. And I kept them for the longest time; I placed them on my shelf wherever I moved. But they disappeared somewhere, I can't remember where.

7. My dad always had a thing for humor. He always tried to crack humor wherever he could. I got in my car once, and he ran outside and knocked on my window. I was done with our meeting; I wanted to leave. And he told me the craziest joke about penguins. I think it was even a knock-knock joke. And he even waddled like a penguin. And I tried to find a laugh somewhere deep inside but I did chuckle. It was a good memory, for him to come outside and knock on my window, besides driving out first of all, and then trying to tell me a joke that he thought was the funniest thing in the world.

8. That he loved me. To this day, he can't stop telling me over the phone when we talk. It kind of seems like that's all he has to say. We started talking over the phone. I used to send him letters.

Because our telephone conversations couldn't be too long, I would record myself on a computer and burn it on a CD. Because I love music, I would send him my favorite songs as well because I knew that he couldn't afford to buy a CD in Mexico. So I would record a two-hour conversation of me as if he were there because also I didn't like typing on the computer, either. But I think he appreciated that more.

Now I have a cell phone and the technology has upgraded; so we are able to talk more frequently and he continues to express his love for me. I never knew that as a child. I thought I was kind of, I guess you would call it, a protégé of him. I had to live in his shadow all the time, and be what he wasn't. There are times when I believe his side of the family looks at me like that. And it's hard to go to events that they have when I am invited, because I see that. But most of all, I want to get on with the conversation; I want to move on, past the point where he's trying to make up for his lost time because there's nothing I or we can do about it.

When we talk, he always tells me when he's lonely, or when he's sad, or even when he's happy. He needs somebody there because he lives in an apartment by himself and he has no one because most of his side of the family lives in San Diego. He says he listens to the CDs and that makes me feel good, because he knows he always has me there, no matter what.


9. Honestly, the memories I have of him are bad. My mom and dad weren't married. He was a beater. He verbally and physically abused my mother in front of me. I can remember two occasions when he almost killed her in front of me. That kind of disturbs me because I can't see why somebody would do that in front of his child.

They're mostly memories of him beating my mom. The salsa was too cold, so he got the whole Tupperware, and threw it against the wall. My mom wanted to leave with me because she was tired of the drama, so he locked the door, grabbed her face with his hands, and threw her on the ground hard. She fell like lumber in a forest. And it was up to me to try and wake her up because he just looked at her, spit on her, and walked away.

I always remember him coming back trying to convince my mom to take him back, and my mom would. I don't remember him sticking up for me. Whenever I had an issue at school, it was always my mom that tried to correct it.

I was around sixteen when he realized that I was at an age that I could think for myself and analyze what was going on. I would confront him about the drug issues and things like that. And I stood up to him. I think that's when he started coming around and trying to make up for things because he knew that I knew what I was talking about.

One time he went to my grandmother's house for refuge because he got jumped, or maybe he was shot. Before this, I had found out my mom had aborted the child before me and I was upset. I felt that my father never stood his ground to have the baby; I always wanted a brother and sister.

I went over there and walked into the room where he was lying; his face was bruised and he looked like a marshmallow. And I was yelling at him, "How could you not do anything?" And I remember him looking at me and rolling over to the TV, and he wouldn't answer me. I said, "We can stay here all night. I have all the time in the world. I just need answers."

And he sat up on the bed and he yelled at me, "What do you want me to say?" All I could think of was that we were two lions guarding our territory.

And I was asking him, "Why didn't you fight it? Why didn't you do anything?" And all he could do was give excuses, saying it was my mom's decision.

All the memories I have are mostly bad memories. They're not good memories and when they are, they are very selective.

*10.* Understanding. Fathers need to understand first of all that they are creating a human being from scratch. They really have control of everything about the way that child turns out. If fathers had a better understanding of that, female and male children would turn out a lot different and for the better.

My dad never had understanding. It was his way or the highway. He's doing a lot better now.

# CHAPTER 53

# Norman

*1.* Norman, and I'm forty-seven.

*2.* I call him Dad a lot of times, but ever since he became a grandfather, he started calling me Uncle Norman and I sometimes call him Grandpa. But I also refer to him as Yo Pop on occasion. It's fluid. But it's always mirthful, because my dad has a great sense of humor.

*3.* Dad has a great sense of humor. My brothers-in-law describe him as the hardest working man in America because my mom wants things just so. She was an only child and she is a princess in her own mind and my dad has treated her that way for fifty years.

The other thing that people tend to remark about my dad is that for eighty years old, he's in good shape. He'll jump off the roof into the pool at my house, and stuff like that.

Yeah, yeah. He's corny to the max. He's always positive, always positive.

*4.* My dad was in the Army when he was younger. He was in World War II. I always remember him saying, "You should always be nice to people because you never know when they'll end up being your sergeant." In more contemporary terms, that means that they could end up being your boss at a later time.

Another thing I always remember him saying is that if you

have a lot of calls to make, always start with the hardest one. Do the hardest one first, and for the rest of the day, the calls are easy.

I also remember him waking me up as a kid, "Up and at 'em. We're burning daylight!" It's like you're wasting time; you should always be doing something.

5. It's funny because my dad was kind of a big shot when I was growing up, but I was sort of in that counter-cultural mode and thought he was a square. My dad was an international banker. I didn't respect or even admire that he was one of the people that helped get MasterCard off and going in Europe and helped enlist a bunch of banks to all honor this one card.

Just recently I prepared a DVD of him to commemorate their fiftieth wedding anniversary. And in going back over the fifty years and seeing all these things that he did, such as him working for the government and traveling all over the world, I just discovered that my dad was a hell of a lot cooler than I ever gave him credit for. He's a pretty cool guy. It reminds me of the Mark Twain expression which I don't recall exactly, but something to the effect that, "When I was thirteen I thought my dad was an idiot, and by the time I was eighteen, I couldn't believe how much smarter he'd gotten."

The older I get, the more I realize how impressive he is.

6. (Immediately.) Sense of humor. It's always okay to laugh. He was never afraid to stick his neck out and be accused of being a little corny. It's always okay to try and kid around a little bit.

7. One of my favorite times was when I was in high school, and I got in trouble. We all went to a psychiatrist as a family and the guy counseled us; then my dad and I spent some time together. We went backpacking in Yosemite for seven days. The first day out, we got hit by bears pretty bad; they devastated our food supply. I thought that meant we needed to turn back, but my dad was completely unfazed. He took the little fishing stuff that we had and sewed our backpacks together. Then we set all our food out and ra-

tioned it. I think having to go through that adversity together was really cool. I always think about that.

And then just recently, I went with him to Washington where he used to work, and he showed me his little bachelor pad in Georgetown. He showed me where he proposed to my mom. He shared the house with four other guys, and proposed in this little alley behind the house for privacy. It just really put a human face on some of his earlier years and made me realize what his life was like then.

The trips that I've taken with him are what I remember most.

*8.* I always thought my mother was more religious than my father because when they got married, my dad had to agree to raise the kids as Catholics. They attend Catholic church and my dad does not receive communion. But then I found out from my mom that my dad believes in an afterlife and my mom does not. I'd always assumed that both parents were extremely religious and bought the whole Catholic dogma—hook, line, and sinker. I guess I'm surprised at the depth of my father's faith; I didn't realize it was that strong. I didn't realize it was stronger than my mom's.

*9.* The clearest one is just recently having been to Washington with him. We drove up the Atlantic seaboard together and had a lot of chances to talk. One of my nephews was there, his grandson, and so we had three generations together. It was interesting, me acting as an intermediary when talking about music with the grandchild. And then when my dad and I would discuss public policy issues of the day, I turned around and explained those to the grandson.

We did this trip just a couple months ago. Seeing where he proposed to my mom, where he lived, and where he worked, was surrounded by their fiftieth wedding anniversary. That prompted the video, which showed the entire backdrop of his life. So it's all sort of intertwined. Being able to look back on his life, I came to the realization that he was a lot cooler guy than I am, and certainly cooler than I ever gave him credit for.

I took still pictures of our trip. In fact, we recreated the marriage proposal. Standing in for my mom was my nephew, and Dad got on one knee. That picture is now one of the more famous pictures in our family, and is circulating through emails.

*10.* Integrity. Practice what you preach. You can't be a leader to a son unless you walk the talk. We lived all over the world and my dad always told us, "You need to treat everyone fairly." And I saw it in his life. The man does not have a prejudiced bone in his body and I've seen him interact with people from countless different ethnicities; he's a man of honor to all of them. He looks for the goodness in people.

It's ironic too, because as political correctness has moved forward, my dad is often victimized as being an old guy that's not with it; he'll forget to refer to the handicapped as handicapped and say, "Oh that's a crippled parking spot for the cripples." And my mother yells at him. His speech may not be politically correct, but his heart has always been there from the beginning. I think the world has caught up with him.

# CHAPTER 54

# Randy

*1.* My name is Randy and my age is forty-seven.

*2.* It was always Dad, and I don't remember anything being different.

*3.* Very outgoing. The life of every party. Crazy sense of humor. Good athlete. Somewhat unfocused. I think I got them all.
Sure. Sure.

*4.* At one point my dad owned a liquor store downtown. I was in sixth grade and I'd been going to basketball camps. He had a lot of trouble running the liquor store. He was the perfect front man, but he wasn't the right businessman to make it successful.

All summer long, I went to an open gym at Saint Mary's where the Phoenix Suns were working out. When open gym ended each day, I took the bus or walked the two miles to my dad's store. After I'd been going there a while, some of the players started giving me rides.

There was this one great guy, Lamar Green. He was a great athlete and had limited common sense; he drove the loudest pink Cadillac I've ever seen in my life. He started giving me rides to the liquor store and that went on for a while. He never came inside; so finally my dad told me I had to have him stop in.

So the next time, Lamar came in. I introduced him to my dad, and he was looking around. And my dad said, "I really appreciate you taking care of my boy and I want to show you how much. Look around. Anything you want, grab it. It's yours." So in perfect form, Lamar took two of the cheapest bottles of wine, not because that's what he liked, but because he was just being nice.

So afterwards my dad says, "Take care of people. Find out what they want. That's the way you say thank you. You find that special something, and that's what you do."

5. Dad died of cancer, and the way he handled all that was incredible. My mom and dad, kind of like my wife and I, are very different, very opposite. As undriven as he was, she was completely driven. And they were always fighting.

There was one particular occasion that was hysterically funny afterwards, not to them I suppose, but always to me. The fight was about preparing cupcakes for my school, and she totally blew up. And it wasn't about cupcakes. It was about all the other crazy things in her life that she wanted to happen, but weren't happening, and he wasn't helping. It was one of the few times that he didn't respond in kind. He just sat back and took the blow.

I asked him about it afterwards, and he said, "You just have to learn at some point—some battles you fight and some you don't."

I was proud of him, there.

6. We're just totally different, opposite personalities. The easy one is love of reading. He always wanted to be a teacher and kept trying to be a businessman, and it never worked out; he never should have tried it. So I guess that was the gift. I realized that part of us was the same; I could try to make a million bucks and it would probably never work out. Not that I'd ever make it, but it wouldn't mean anything anyway.

I did the law thing. I have a law degree. I was working for the Tucson County Attorney's office. I had a job and a contract in Albuquerque and literally at the twelfth hour, I turned the law job down and decided I was going to go back and get my Master's degree. I didn't even know if I would teach at that point. And then, I went off in that direction.

I grew up in Albuquerque. The father of the family I grew up with was a big attorney; he had four adopted kids and they all turned out to be tragedies. He was handing me the key and wanted me to take it. But it wouldn't have worked out.

7. I could tell all kinds of sports stories because we did a lot of that. Two come to mind.

He was always working two jobs, so the time that we could actually go and do things was limited. So one day in the middle of the summer, he just grabbed me and said, "Let's go down and I'll throw batting practice and you can hit." He knew I was struggling in Little League with my hitting. So it was a hundred-and-ten degrees in the middle of June and we went down to the field.

I'd asked him before, "I just have my bat. I don't have a helmet."

He said, "You're all right. I've got a great arm and I'm not going to throw it hard."

So we got out there; it was hotter that hell, and I didn't want to be there. First pitch, he beaned me. (Laughs.) And he almost, not quite, knocked me out; I did black out and I was scared to death. He rushed me home and then he called my mom with the whole thing. It was funny.

My other favorite story was about their huge Christmas party. It was a part social, part family thing. My mom invited most of the people. So Mom and Dad had spent all night making her favorite chocolate candies. They were so tired by the time of the party, but my mom put on her game face and she was in great form, very directed.

I walked in and saw my dad eating all these candies.

"What are you doing? You stayed up!" I said.

"Well, they're all filled with rum," he said and he ate them for a half hour. He was blasted. In the middle of the party, he got two blocks of wood and nailed them together with hangers, and built an impromptu ukulele. Then he got up and sang to all the people at the party. And absolutely (Laughs), just (Laughs)—it was so outrageous. I think he would have done it without the rum candies. But, it was perfect. It was his release. It was his revenge.

*8.* We had really good communications. And then of course he was terminal for two years, so we talked about everything. I don't think there was anything afterwards, not really.

The only bizarre thing was he was completely non-violent, non-aggressive as well as non-violent. He grew up in Long Beach, California. Now it's a crime-ridden urban area, but he said back then it was just a little village on the ocean.

One time he went to a park with a small group of three or four guys. They went into a public restroom and there was a guy in there molesting a kid. They all got in a fight. Dad said he damn near cut the guy up, but didn't. But it was just that close. He said it was the only time in his life that he ever felt that way. I was a little surprised by that. The dad I knew never would have felt something like that, even if defending his own household; if somebody broke into our house, he would have told a few jokes first.

*9.* We went to Disneyland one summer, and they had just finished It's A Small World. And for whatever reason, one of the things that stuck with Dad is that they had evergreen trees and bushes that they had grown and trimmed into animal shapes. We had three similar trees in our back yard.

After we got back from Disneyland, Dad had me follow him out to the hedges. And he told me, "We're going to shape our trees like animals."

And I wanted to say, "You are so full of shit. You don't have any idea what you're doing."

So we butchered them. But we had a great time. We just completely butchered those trees. But it was Disneyland. (Laughs.) He was so outlandish. (Laughs.)

*10.* I think ultimately, incredible patience. Take the long view. Don't take things personally from your kids. Try to keep in mind what you hope that final relationship looks like. Stay patient. Try to make it happen.

CHAPTER 55

# Timothy

*1.* Timothy, fifty-five.

*2.* I called him Dad. And I really don't know how it evolved.

*3.* My father was stoic; he showed very little emotion. But his inner warmth was there even if he didn't show much emotion to people. He was a listener instead of a talker, took things in. But when he contributed, he always had something clever and witty to say. But he didn't share very often. That was one of the qualities about him I admired because I was so different and I wished I was more like that.

I agree a hundred percent. Sometimes it felt a little difficult to get close to him, but I always knew that he cared and he was always there. And there was always an inner warmth, although a lot of times you had to look hard to see through the shell.

*4.* I was kind of a self-starter. I remember my father teaching me how to cast a fishing rod and reel. We spent a couple long afternoons on the bank trying to get me to do it with some sort of skill. I spent a lot of time with it hung up in trees, but he was always very patient.

I don't think I was a very good listener because I thought I pretty much knew everything. But his patience spoke volumes when we did things together; he seemed to always be able to accept my failures without a lot of criticism. He was very supportive in his own way. He taught me things more by omission; the things I learned were by a glance that he'd give me. I could read him like a book. A certain look and I'd be in tears. Another look, and I'd be elated. He could fire me up or ice me out with just a quick glance. That was how he showed his affection, in looks, and with a certain way he had of putting me in my place without raising a hand or his voice.

5. The things that I was proud of my father about were kind of simple things like his responsibility. He would never miss work; he would never be late. He was a man of his word. I think that's why I was most proud of him. I learned responsibility from him, not from a lot of words and a lot of actions, but based on observing how he ran his life and his personal business. Sometimes he could procrastinate, but he was always to work on time. He took the things that were important in his life very seriously. I was proud of him for that.

Where some men would drink and chase women and do other things that would cause families to suffer in some way, my dad was always there. He always did what he was supposed to do. He was somebody who would never break the rules, no improprieties of any kind. He was a straight shooter and a straight arrow. And I was proud of him for that. Just the way he conducted his life made me proud of him. He was very responsible and he was a good model.

6. The way I fathered my children was a direct reflection of the way my father fathered me. I didn't lay hands on my kids. I didn't have to; I gave them the look. The look was enough, enough said. It stopped them in their tracks and put them into tears. They knew exactly where I was coming from and how I felt by that look. Either the warmth or the coldest of my feelings were felt and that's what I got from him.

You don't have to yell and scream and beat people to get your point across. You drive it home a lot more clearly if you do it with a few words and with a lot of feeling and emotion. I think whatever leadership qualities I developed were reflections of him. And

I wished I'd been more like him in terms of being a little more reticent to talk. A lot of times I would have learned a lot more things by listening, but I always kind of led with my chin. He hung back more, and did things a little more wisely. Where fools rush in. What I picked up from my father was how to deal with people and the world in an effective way—how to treat people with respect and get what you want without having to beat them over the head with it.

7. It was pretty unusual to see my father and I walking anywhere because my dad was five foot eight and I was six foot five. I was almost double his height and double his girth. A lot of people even had difficulty believing that I was his son because of that disparity in size.

We had a kindred spirit and kindred hearts. We looked so different and we were very different. But the deeper you'd cut, probably the more we were alike; that's what I'm finding out later in life. I really am my father. I hope I'm just a bigger, louder version of the same character.

8. After my father passed away, I learned from my mother's stories that there were times when he was dissatisfied with something I'd done or said, although he didn't convey it to me. She told me several things about my father that he felt and didn't say. Evidently, he wanted my mother to be the person who would be the disciplinarian. And that kind of surprised me; I'm not sure if it's even true because I think she knew that I favored my father. And that was a way after his death, for her to maybe gain some of my confidence, or more of my respect.

I think the most telling thing was when I left to go to the University of Nevada at Las Vegas on a scholarship. The day I left, we stood out by my car. And as I started to drive away, my father just broke up in tears. And I cried for the first fifty miles going down the road as I was leaving home for the first time.

Two times I saw my father in tears. The other was when I was eleven years old and having surgery. My first Little League game I threw a no-hitter. And after the game, they had to rush me to the hospital. I was in tremendous abdominal pain; I had an appendicitis attack. And as they were wheeling me off on a gurney into the operating room, I looked up at my father; our eyes met, and he just broke up. I knew something was really serious because I'd never seen that kind of emotion from him. And that was the exact same reaction he had later when I drove off to college.

He had such a depth of feeling and we didn't see it very often. And when we did, it was so profound, it was almost painful to feel that kind of intensity.

9. The times when we hunted and fished together. I remember a time when we he and I went deer hunting. We were at a place called Cordes Junction, back in the wilderness. He and I had been hunting for two and a half days, tramping through brush and everything else, and we sat in this little clearing and waited. A deer came running out and we both aimed and shot at the exact same instant. It was like one shot. I thought I just shot; he thought he just shot. The deer fell, and we made the kill. We were both so happy and neither one of us knew who fired the kill; there was only one hit. (Laughs.) It never mattered, because we didn't compete against each other. It was all for one, one for all.

Those are the times I remember with the most warmth— watching him catch a fish. When Dad was an eighteen year old high school senior, he joined the Navy during the Second World War and he got rheumatic fever in boot camp. He was flat on his back for almost six months and it damaged his heart; the rest of his life he got a small pension from the government. So he was never a hundred percent or really physically able to do a lot of things. And his life was just kind of a deterioration, slowly but surely, and he died at fifty-three years of age because of his heart disease. So we never got to have the richness of life we probably would have had without that. The times that I remember most and best are the ones that we spent together out in nature with a gun or with a fishing pole—just those kinds of simple things.

I do remember a great story though, now that I'm thinking about it. We were at a place up on the Mogollion Rim called Knoll

Lake, a beautiful trout lake. He and I caught almost a hundred trout in three days. We were just slaying them. And we're lying there one night, and I heard this clomping, chewing sound. I opened up the tent flap and there was a great big bear eating our groceries and smashing our ice chest. So I start looking around. We had a twenty-two pistol in the tent, and I was struggling around for it.

And my dad said, "What are you doing?"

And I said, "I'm gonna get him Dad!"

And he said, "Don't move. Shut up!" And he kind of held me down and we just sat there and watched as this bear destroyed our camp and then lumbered off. My brashness probably would have gotten us both killed. I just remember how he protected me then; he always had the wisdom that he needed to get us through anything. I was always a little bit too eager and he was the mellowing influence that always kept me out of danger.

*10.* I think fathers need to be extremely patient, which mine was. I wish I had his patience. Fathers need the ability to let children make their own mistakes and go their own way, guide a little if asked for advice, but be patient and let them go their own way.

And keep your nose out of other people's business. He was a perfect example of that. I don't think he ever offered, or in any way was ever overbearing or rude. I've never seen him act inappropriately. I admired his ability and his patience to let people screw up all they wanted. He may have had thoughts about it, and you'd hear about it later, but he would never stick his nose in other people's business or tell people how to act or what they should do. Live and let live was his motto.

I think patience is the greatest virtue that people can have with other people. And I learned that from him. I don't always have it, but he did.

# What: My Take

Never underestimate how important a father is. Mathew is right.

Dads make a difference. The stories and memories shared by the Fifty-Five confirm this fact; fathers mean a lot to their families, and often mean much more to the sons. The relationship a son has to his father is probably his most primal and powerful connection in his life. And sons remember. They remember the good and the bad. And some of the bad they even remember as good, because time together is still good even if the weather, or the score, or the advice isn't. Time is precious. Time spent together equals love.

Time is the key, even though it might seem to be a generational thing. Some of the older Fifty-Five described fathers being too busy to play or guide. Earlier generations lived through the scraping and the pains of the Depression and working fathers were often too busy and too worn out for play time. Because of that and other factors, many of the boomers and the newer generations of fathers have tried to connect with their own children on a more personal level. Jet said that his generation was more open-minded and talked with their kids more. But it all comes down to time. How much kids-only time is planned and really spent? Sons remember time spent together because that's when bonds are created.

Time together is also when questions get aired and when dads can teach values and skills. Time together can be time spent learning how to change a tire, read a book, gut a fish, learn to drive, chainsaw firewood, weld, or run a business. Or maybe just to ask, "Are you feeling better today?" All together moments are teachable moments, moments when you can teach values and problem-solving skills that will stay with kids forever. Carl's dad taught safety while they were firing the cannon. The grocery store is an excellent time and place to discuss counting, colors, money, food preparation, farming, budgeting, bioethics, marketing, or whatever you want.

When we were kids, we learned by watching and listening to our elders. Sometimes we were lucky enough to have someone older and wiser that took the time to explain and show us how to do things in this world. And if we were very lucky, that person was also a storyteller. It is sometimes said that storytelling is a lost art, but the Fifty-Five prove that to be far from correct. Storytellers pass on unique family traditions, favorite stories, funny stories, and examples of good and bad.

Sons really remember time together. Memories are so precious and special but which ones stand out, and why? Times shared in repeated daily routines or in special one-to-one experiences seem to be remembered more. Leonard and others said it best—being there is the most important. John always smiles when he remembers his dad's worried face right after the dog knocked him down while playing Frisbee.

Being together, working on the day-to-day stuff like Alfred helping his father on the farm counts a lot. Clark spent quality time with his ailing dad at Wal-Mart and while cutting wood. Even being miserable together counts because it's still being together. Blake told about his awful, hiking-in-the-rain camping trip as a terrible hike, but a happy memory of a good time together with his dad.

If you want most men to talk, you have to ask questions—questions that need more than a yes or no answer. Men sometimes won't initiate a conversation, but they will answer if you ask. If someone else needs attention, most men will stand aside; if it's not our turn, we wait. Start with easy questions to warm up before you ask the big ones. And be ready to listen patiently.

Listen more, talk less; Randolph was right. Always listen first. Kids and most men will talk if you ask and then back up a little and wait; they will respond. Give them space to answer. But you have to be patient. Listening to them will help you figure how to help make your time together the most powerful it can be. Listen first. Breathe. Talk briefly. Listen more.

And be in the moment; keep your focus on the person and on the ideas you are discussing. Don't think about what you might say next; keep your focus on listening and connecting. Some of those times may even become teachable moments when you can help a kid grasp a concept right there in front of your eyes, like Doug does when he gets around kids and gets a chance to talk about what kind of bird it is and where it lives.

Kids need skills. Each generation must take the time and embrace the chances to pass skills on. Telling our family stories keeps our family traditions and our ancestors alive in our children's hearts. Kids want to connect to something bigger. That's a big part of what this book is all about. Tell your stories of dreaming, stumbling, building, and achieving your dreams.

Doing things together creates the most lasting kind of connection. The optimum conditions might be just the two of you in a place new to one or both of you. It might be the dad helping the kid explore a new world; Bob's dad took him along to New Orleans for a convention. It's about undivided attention. Those fishing, hiking, camping, hunting, driving, swimming, playing places really stand out in the Fifty-Five's memories and stories. The special events seem more memorable because they are strongly linked emotionally to the situations and people. Travel can be very revealing, both because of larger blocks of time together, and because of the physical nearness of it. It also requires lots of thinking on your feet and survival skills, as Joshua explained.

Privacy and a new place can be helpful, but it doesn't need to be anything special other than time together talking and sharing our stories, skills, and experiences. Anywhere. Any time of day or night. Just be together.

Place and time do connect for memories, as do kindness and stepping up. For James Louis, it was going with his dad to his grandpa's to spend quiet working time to shut down his grandpa's house after his grandpa's death. For Clark, it was finally using the chainsaw rather than the flashlight. For Lee, it was watching his dad jump in the lake wearing his brown three-piece business suit to show them all that he would do exactly as he pleased. For Killbird, it was his step-dad shouldering all the father jobs.

Sixteen of the men had strong memories of times spent fishing; Brent, Lee, James Louis, Jay, James, Neb, and ten others all shared fishing stories. Fishing came up more than any other single activity. Kenneth said fishing was really important to him because it was the only thing he and his father had in common. Fishing is time away in isolation and might also fit as a survive-it-together experience. Once you get camped and all set up, fishing leaves a lot of time to listen, talk, and reflect. Fishing is a perfect time together away experience on all levels—so it makes sense that it surfaced in so many stories.

The Fifty-Five also focused on the quality of time; time should be well spent and not wasted. Johnny fondly recalls time spent working with his dad on his car—time really listening to each other while doing something together. Joshua also refers to this while discussing his hiking trip with his son before his son went into the Marines; they had time to really talk to each other. Harvey said golfing allowed plenty of time to get past the pleasantries and on to the important discussions. Bob shared quality time with his dad while his dad taught him how to be a quality craftsman.

All of us are role models. Families watch and listen to the others around them for cues of behavior and decision-making. Sons plan to be the alpha-male some day, somewhere, and watching Dad is on-the-job training. Michael was proud of his dad and wanted to grow up and work with him. Tom, John Henry, and Andrew were very proud of their minister fathers. So we listen and watch, and we learn with our ears and our eyes. We remember things others do. We also remember the things we do with others. Everyone is watching.

Kenneth said that men change when they become fathers. Most become more conscious of the world and our children's place in the future, and we start questioning people's behavior in front of the kids. We become more responsible, just as Clark, Dave and others said. We find ourselves thinking more about the long-range consequences of our actions and modeling what we want. At our best, we become better men and fathers when we see life through the eyes of the people we love.

Some role models showed up as real heroes. Jet's father grabbed Jet before he spun out the open car door as they drove down the street. After his cross-country car trip with his eighty-year-old dad, Norman realized that his father was much cooler than he had ever thought possible. Wes recalled how his father kept a dangerous drunk away from a school bus of kids. Joshua's fifty year old Tata fell out of a tree and climbed back up there to shake out those pinon nuts as the grandkids called him Superman. Michael's dad sprung Michael from jail. Killbird's dad even pulled Killbird's brother out from an old well shaft, golf clubs and all.

Add to the list of heroes men like Andrew's dad and Michael's dad and Killbird's dad who chose to accept the responsibility of being a father to make sure their boys were raised with good values and experiences. Any man with good intentions who steps up to help father and mentor a kid is a heavenly addition to our world. Heroes come in many packages, and none are more valued than a step-dad or surrogate father.

Some people are not good role models, and end up being anti-role models; they exhibit the opposite of good behavior. Johnny recalled his dad's swearing to be a bad example and Johnny doesn't swear. Tommy's dad told him to steal big, but Tommy is and was far from a thief. For Diego it was absorbing impatience at home. The Fifty-Five spoke often of distant, too busy fathers, and said they would have liked more quality time with their dads when they were kids. Some even had fathers that left the home and the family.

Most men won't show emotions easily, if at all. "Keep your cards close to your chest." We're built that way. "Be strong; don't let them know how you feel on the inside." It's not easy for men to show their emotions. "Stop your blubbering, you baby." And when men do show their feelings, it's often considered weak or ineffective.

Lee, Bob, Jerry, Jet, and Michael all referred to their dads as being sensitive, which is a code word for showing outward signs of emotion. Others referred to emotional situations generally without using a descriptive term. A wide range of emotional responses seems to be bundled up in the word sensitive. Having a code word itself shows how men sometimes hide from feelings, which is why real sorrow and troubles can often cut men at the knees. Many men don't know how to handle the emotions that accompany bad times; many don't even have other men they can really talk to. And as Raphael points out, most men are disconnected to their feminine side, which makes it even more challenging for males and females to understand each other and live together happily.

Men and women are wired differently. We really don't see the same things or see them in the same way. Men will read these stories to get clarification, validation, and maybe advice. Men, may these stories ring true to your experiences and possibly shed some light on our connection to being men. Women will read them to see what the heck is going in men's minds. Ladies, after you are done reading, carefully ask your man some questions. He'll talk to you; you just have to start the ball rolling and wait for his answer. Give him time to think, and be ready to listen patiently.

My take is that fathers are very important. I have always believed this, but my time with the Fifty-Five and their stories is complete confirmation. The power I have gained from sharing their personal stories has given me an opportunity to deeply explore my own feelings. I am feeling more sensitive. I have been pulled in and some great old memories and family stories have resurfaced. I have a deeper awareness that we all must continue to plan more time together with our loved ones. I still love and miss my dad more every day. After all these years, I find myself turning to him for advice and counsel and then, oh yeah, he's gone. But he's not; I remember things he said and shared and it helps. We all live on in our memories of the times we spend together.

Here's a list of ten things that my experiences with the Fifty-Five have etched in my brain. Thank you for reading. I sincerely hope that sharing these stories and ideas will help you be closer with all your loved ones, especially the men in your life.

☞ 1. Love conquers all. It really does. Your cooking or your money or your car may be part of what draws your kids to you, but what they really want is your love and they look forward to any chance to get more.

☞ 2. Take every opportunity to listen and talk to your kids. This kind of quality time can be driving to school, at dinner, or while shopping at Home Depot. Listen. Share. Find out what is going on and with whom. Stay connected to their lives by being there. Your kids want you to care and to be there. Create a happy, connected life together by using your feet, your time, and your energy.

☞ 3. Grab any teachable moments that happen when you are with your kids. Weave real life lessons and values into regular events or conversations; you might even include a family story. If something breaks around the house and you fix it, let your son carry tools or even assist you while you explain what's going on or just talk about what's for dinner. It could be business or girlfriends, TV or sports; but share your ideas and boundaries through explanations and examples. You can be doing almost anything together and talking about almost anything else—it's your chance to pull him up to a higher level of understanding.

☞ 4. Pass on your skills and your stories. Share your knowledge. Somebody taught you. Many of us are visual learners; witness the huge attraction to computers. Do people read the user's manual for those new gadgets or games? No, they just dive in and try it. Jay reminds us that a mentor's guiding hand can make a big difference in learning any skill. Some people know cars or farming or plumbing or carpentry or gardening. Each of us adds to the collective knowledge of everyone we touch in our lives. Pass it on. Teach a man to fish; you know the rest.

Everybody loves stories. That's how we connect to examples of strength and goals, good behaviors and love. It's also how we connect to people that are far away or deceased. Tell your stories and be silly or noisy, and make faces and voices; we love it when you let your guard down and just be goofy while you share tales of special people and how they live in this world. And please, pass your stories on. Tell your kids your family stories. They want to hear them and they'll love you more for it.

☞ 5. Praise your kids' good work and effort. Always plant positive ideas, pictures, and associations in your kids' minds. As Joshua said, always be positive and never underestimate a kid's potential. If you could choose to talk to someone who always found your mistakes, or you could talk to someone who praised your effort and accomplishments, which person would you talk to? Be the person your kid wants to talk to. Always accent the positive.

Clayton teased his daughter that he mustn't be such an ogre if her friends came around to talk with him. Try to downplay bad choices and outcomes by focusing on good efforts and goals. Kids want to please their parents, and when we praise them we give them the opportunity to do so, which builds a path to continued closeness and trust. Be the person you would pick to trust.

☞ 6. Time together is what counts. Nothing is as important as time together listening and talking. Randolph said real listening equals respect. One-on-one time stays deeper in memory. Want to get closer to your kid? Design situations where you can be together, like John's dad did when he took John to the plant on Saturday, or like Jason's dad did when Jason and he did the grocery shopping each Sunday. Chief talked about his joy at just having coffee and breakfast alone with his dad before they continued construction of the porch. Plan and spend time with the people you love. Make time together happen.

☞ 7. Bad time is still time together. Blake's bad hiking trip, Timothy's brush with a bear, and Tommy's scary roof's edge conversation with his dad are all examples of good times spent doing not so good things. So even if your planned outing together went wrong, you still got the together part right and surviving the adversities might even create a deeper bond between the two of you.

☞ 8. Practice unconditional love. Tell your son you love him. Tell your dad you love him. Show him even more. Carlos, Mathew, James and others were very specific about this. And accept love. Let him know he can screw up and you'll still love him. Period. Let him know when you don't like his choices, but at the same time, let him know that you always love him. Let them know how proud you are. Love him unconditionally and allow him to love you back unconditionally.

☞ 9. Randy said it best. Take the long view. Don't take things personally from your kids. Keep in mind what you hope that final relationship will be like.

☞ 10. Be patient. Be extra patient. When I asked for the single trait every dad should have in his bag of tricks, patience came up most often. And patience fits perfectly with forgiveness and unconditional love. Many of the stories show how being patient, forgiving, and loving were the right choices because things worked out. Rather than wasting time worrying, patience shows trust in the people and the situations. Quite often, things do work out.

Trust in the love and the values you have given each other. It will help you be patient as life unfolds around you and your loved ones.

# Fifty-Five Favorite Strengths Fast

Here's the fast version of all Fifty-Five men's answers to *Question Ten: What single trait or strength should all fathers own?*

As long as you let the child know that you love them, care about them, and allow them to become the person they are going to be, you'll be a good father.

The thing that I like the most about my dad is that I can communicate with him; he listens and doesn't just automatically react to whatever is said.

It would be that they have more connection to home life, to being there with the family. Obviously dads made tons of mistakes like everyone does, but I think when it comes down to it, you've got to always feel like you can count on your dad.

Patience. Don't avoid issues. And refrain from laying guilt trips.

I think a sense of obligation and responsibility to your children and to your wife, and then of respect and love.

Their strength should be love, which fathers do, but not all of them. That's one thing dad taught us—respect.

A father must be a provider for his kids, teach them right and wrong, and teach them how to love and just be there for them, no matter what.

You need to be there for your kids. Growing from a kid into a good adult isn't something that happens automatically.

Gentle kindness is a huge strength. I don't think kids appreciate kindness as a strength until they are in the position of being a father.

Have an open mind and be able to accept your children as they are. Show patience and understanding and let them grow up to be their own person.

Don't overtly show disappointment in behavior that doesn't quite come up to par. So patience. Patience. The same patience that I would hope God shows to us. You know we screw up.

A son has to believe in his father. The son has to believe what he does, and what he thinks, and what he wants.

Be stern about your kids. You have to be. It's the only way they are going to be raised right. Like they say, we are raising leaders.

I guess he had the right amount of being strict and the right amount of compassion, caring, and love, while not spoiling us.

You need to have a lot of patience. And be understanding. I think one good trait is you have to listen real close and not make a quick, decisive decision.

I want all fathers to show affection to their kids. Spend time with them, and discipline them, and teach them the correct things while showing them that dad still cares for and loves them.

If the kid gets into any trouble or anything, the father should sit and listen to him and try and help him out.

Dads must keep striving for a goal that they want. For me, I probably wouldn't be at the job I'm at right now if it weren't for my kids. I've got to keep going so I can take care of them.

Dependability, most definitely. Dependability and integrity.

Devotion isn't too strong a word. I think fathers need to have that responsibility toward the family and toward their kids. It isn't necessarily the amount of time that you spend, it's that you have quality time with your kids all through their life. I'd say devotion, dedication. Being there for your kids and your family and making that time quality time, not just a paycheck.

You've got to spend time with your kids. And it's not just being in the room or being there while they're there that's important. I think you have to interact and actually be involved in what they are doing, or have to say, or how they're feeling.

Put the needs and wants of the child first; it's a matter of what's best for them.

I think all fathers should tell their boys how much they love them. Or show it in some way, like my dad did, hug you every morning.

I think it's unconditional love. I can't even think about not having that with my kids.

I advise everybody; keep that courage in yourself so you can survive when you are not with your kids.

Patience. Patience. Because of my father having patience, he has taught me and really made me more patient, over and over again.

Heart. You have to love your kids with all your heart because your kids and life are going to pull at you in a thousand ways. You need that always on, always ready, always accepting kind of love. Heart gives you the focus and endurance to stay strong and stay together.

Honesty. Dads have to be honest with self and be honest with their children and with their family. As long as you have honesty, then you can work anything out.

They should be there. They should encourage their kids to do good things. And encourage them to find a passion and go with it, even if it's something really awkward.

Empathetic. Big time. It's easy to be strong. And it's easy to be firm, which is what a lot of fathers are. But they have to show a different side and say, "I can understand what you're saying."

Love. Patience. Leadership. You've got to be a leader in your own family because your kids need to know that they have a parent that loves them, that means what he says, and supports them.

Fathers can't be too lenient; they have to put their foot down occasionally. Kids need boundaries. Dads have to be the enforcer of the family. So sometimes kids hate fathers, but most of the time he's a good guy.

The two words that sum up my dad would be caring and sharing.

Express your inner feelings of love and caring with the people that you do love and do care for. Men need to break that iceberg demeanor and be able to show the love and the caring that they have. Men need to be able to express love.

I think open-mindedness, caring. Unconditional love is what I think kids need. Just support kids. Love them. And don't be so quick to judge. We shouldn't take these things personally. They're just growing up.

A father can teach so much through the love that he shows with his wife and his children. So often you've got to be a manly man; you've got to be tough, and you've got to be hard-core. A father has to put that to the side and show a soft side of love for his family but still be strong and be very secure with his manhood.

First, unconditional love for their families. Since I've had kids of my own and been married, my wife and kids mean the world to me. You need to put your family as the central focus of your life. Second, would be to love them, be involved in their lives, be interested in what they do, and be part of their lives. Third, a father has to be willing to do whatever it takes to provide for his family.

The ability to be cool when something that doesn't seem so good happens is probably the most important—to collect their thoughts and see what's going on and not be reactionary. As a kid, you expect dad to take whatever happens, rationally deal with it, not freak out, and not do things for the wrong reasons.

I believe that we are a combination of male and female and that too many men never touch on or embrace the feminine. They need to acknowledge it so they'll have better relationships and have a better connection with women. It's up to the fathers to teach that.

I don't think a father ought to bring a child into this world without seeing that child through his education, regardless of the marital circumstances. People don't grow up well in a one-parent environment. And that doesn't just go with the idea of supporting them financially, but it has to do with raising them, and giving them character and substance for all of their life.

I think the fact that he has been stern and up front with me since I was real little makes me appreciate him more now. And it's the way that he's taught me to go about things, as far as what's right and what's wrong. His way of how to go about things and deal with stuff has paid off in dividends.

The duty of a father is to be there, step up, and be responsible. That's part and parcel of loving your kids. You've got to be there to take care of business. And that goes beyond just going to work and making money.

They should be honest and they should be up front with everyone, especially their offspring. They should be a devoted and dedicated parent. Any father, any parent, should be a good listener. They should listen more than they speak.

Patience and hope. You have to be able to understand the uniqueness in each child, and be able to make appropriate adjustments in how you provide the love and the caring that is needed. You also have to understand that there is no one way that's going to work for all of them. Never lose hope, and never communicate that a child is hopeless, or incompetent, or incapable.

The balance of firmness and love—it's got to be there. You have to be the strong hand of the household, but you've got to remember that for every strong moment, you've got to have that moment of praise and show him how much you love him.

To be the best father you can be, the most important things are selflessness and the ability to unconditionally give and receive love. Fathers have to be able to step out of themselves and give and receive unconditional love. Giving love with conditions creates problems; it can influence kids in a negative way if they constantly think that they have to earn love or aren't able to give love. Never under-estimate how important a father is.

I think you've got to be honest and model that for your children while interacting in a consistent fashion. I would say honesty in just being who you are, with all your shortcomings, and not being afraid to acknowledge that they exist.

Forgiveness. Because no matter how perfect kids are, eventually everybody does something wrong sometime. You just can't hold on to it. Sometimes you've just got to bite your tongue and show compassion and forgiveness.

Patience. Patience. There are lots of things I can't do now because my dad didn't teach me because he wasn't patient enough to finish the job. I inherited and mimicked his impatience so I didn't teach myself either. You can't assume that one try is ever going get something done; it's not going to happen.

Understanding. Fathers need to understand first of all that they are creating a human being from scratch. They really have control of everything about the way that child turns out. If fathers had a better understanding of that, all children would turn out a lot different and a lot better.

Integrity. Practice what you preach. You can't be a leader to a son unless you walk the talk.

I think ultimately, incredible patience. Take the long view. Don't take things personally from your kids. Try to keep in mind what you hope that final relationship looks like. Stay patient. Try to make it happen.

I think fathers need to be extremely patient, which mine was. Fathers need the ability to let children make their own mistakes and go their own way; guide a little if asked for advice, but be patient and let them go their own way.

Learn from yesterday, live for today, hope for tomorrow. The important thing is to not stop questioning.

Albert Einstein, father of two

Printed in the United States
95953LV00007B/37/A